Sharing the World's Resources

Sharing the World's Resources

Oscar Schachter

Columbia University Press
New York 1977

Library of Congress Cataloging in Publication Data

Schachter, Oscar, 1915–
    Sharing the world's resources.

    Includes bibliographical references and index.
    1. Natural resources—International cooperation.
    2. Wealth.   3. Social justice.   I. Title.
    Law   341.7′5   76-28422
    ISBN 0-231-04110-1

Columbia University Press
New York   Guildford, Surrey
Copyright © 1977 Columbia University Press
Printed in the United States of America

Preface

THIS book considers the age-old theme of distributive justice in its contemporary application to world affairs. It owes its origin to three lectures given in 1974 at the Northwestern University Law School under the distinguished auspices of the Julius Rosenthal Foundation. In that year the idea of equitable sharing of resources among nations had moved, almost suddenly, to the center of the world's stage. Declarations were adopted in international assemblies calling for a new and just international economic order. Demands for equitable sharing were advanced in numerous international bodies concerned with the use and allocation of common resources or with the distribution of the global product. Not surprisingly, these demands emanated primarily from the poor and disadvantaged. What was more striking is the extent to which they found an affirmative response in the wider international community. Even the rich and the powerful proclaimed their adherence to the principle of equitable sharing and, more significantly, perceived it as related to their own national interest. The disequilibrium in the world economy—the combination of crises over oil, food, inflation, deficits, and recession—had accentuated their sense of dependence on others and deepened their anxieties. In these conditions, a response to demands for economic justice could not be sharply separated from an interest in their own stability and well-being.

It is one of the aims of this book to examine the basic normative issues raised by these demands and their practical application in international decisions. It does this both on the general level of principles of entitlement and on the more specific level of cooperative arrangements and rules to resolve conflicts. The analysis moves from philosophical and juridical concepts to the political, economic, and institutional factors which influence international behavior. The book's main object is to throw light on the ways in which the abstract ideal of equitable sharing can be given determinate meaning and political acceptability. It also aims at a better understanding of the diverse international structures and procedures which affect the division of the world's wealth. Collective decision making is examined in a variety of situations with particular reference to the conflicts and the dilemmas presented by the demands for equitable sharing. Law, viewed broadly as a process of decision, is treated as a significant instrument both for clarifying international objectives and for facilitating rational choices. But its role is seen as part of the wider political and social context, not as an autonomous force.

Obviously, this is not a comprehensive treatise on international law and practice relating to the distribution of global resources. Though I deal with a broad range of problems, my principal focus is on emerging ideas and principles and their use in meeting the demands for greater equity and economic well-being. Lengthy description has been avoided and complicated topics have been treated with brevity. (However, extensive footnote references have been included, particularly to documentary source material that is often overlooked.) It is hoped that the relatively concise treatment of current issues in a wide variety of contexts will enable the reader to perceive more clearly the significant normative criteria and the principal dilemmas presented by the demands for a new and just international economic order.

It seemed especially fitting to select this theme for the 1974 Rosenthal Lectures, not only because of its contemporary interest but in view of the contribution which that distinguished series of lectures has made to understanding the significance of justice and the role played by law in its pursuit. It was indeed a great privilege for me to join the eminent company of Rosenthal lecturers, and I am especially grateful to Dean James Rahl and Professors Jay Hillman, Brunson MacChesney, and Nathaniel Nathanson for interest and encouragement. The several days spent at Northwestern Law School with faculty, students, and alumni are memorable both for lively intellectual exchange and the warmth of friendly contacts. My subsequent revision and expansion of the lectures for this book were stimulated by the comments there as well as by the ferment and developments on the international scene.

I am grateful to the United Nations Institute for Training and Research (UNITAR) for the opportunity to work on this book while I was associated with the Institute. Dr. Davidson Nicol, its present executive director, was generous in his encouragement of my effort in this as in other studies, and I am greatly indebted to him. I am also indebted to Dr. Karel Vosskühler (now of the Netherlands Foreign Service) and Miss Margaret Croke of UNITAR for valuable research assistance in obtaining source material on some aspects of the book. My friends and colleagues, Drs. Sanford Schwarz, K. V. Raman, and Aida Levin were most helpful in sharing their knowledge and insights. No one, however, merits more appreciation than my wife whose encouragement and good sense were invaluable.

Oscar Schachter
December 1975

Contents

Sharing the World's Resources

Part I
International
Equity and
Its Dilemmas

PROBLEMS of equitable sharing among nations are not new. They have arisen for centuries in regard to boundary waters, fisheries, and the terms of trade. But the scale and intensity of such problems are vastly greater today; they permeate the domestic economies and social life of almost all countries, and they have generated a widespread consciousness of inequalities and dependencies that is surely unprecedented. In the 1970s this has been sharply accentuated by imbalances and scarcities which threaten to destroy the social fabric of many areas and which, even in the most prosperous countries, have reversed the long-prevalent idea of continuous material progress.

It is mainly because of these conditions that some international bodies may be said to have become "justice-constituencies," arenas in which claims of equity and distributive justice are asserted and "internationalized." [1] These bodies vary widely. Some are concerned in concrete ways with allocation of goods or prices; others with access to resources; others, more generally, with cooperative arrangements over a range of economic and social matters (as, for example, the European Economic Community or the Andean organization). They are often specialized or regional organs which lay down rules and standards relevant to allocation of resources or carry out operational and managerial functions that affect the distribution of goods and services. More conspicuous are the general international bodies, typified by the General Assembly of the United Nations and its Conference on Trade and Development (UNCTAD), which are almost continuously engaged in considering demands for more equitable treatment and in formulating collective responses of a normative character. These generally take the form of declarations, charters, and resolutions, often couched in terms of rights and obligations. Whether or not they are accepted as international legal rules, they are likely to engender expectations about future patterns of international distribution, and, in some cases, to delegitimize traditional norms which would otherwise be regarded as authoritative. In that way multilateral conferences and international organs influence the development of customary international law even though they are not explicitly engaged in lawmaking efforts.

Although this may seem surprising, there is actually no sharp line separating the normative judgments of many international bodies from the continuous and ubiquitous process of customary law creation that takes place through the interaction of states.[2] An essential element of that process is the common perception of right and obligation on the part of the states concerned; when such shared perceptions emerge and are expressed clearly in international bodies, they are bound to shape the development of legal norms. All in all, there are a variety of international structures in which demands for equitable distribution may be made and given authoritative force by collective decisions. By examining these collective decisions we can discern the emergence of the normative concepts and criteria which bear on the sharing of the world's wealth. My aim in this book is to examine these emergent concepts and criteria and to consider their practical implications for the resolution of international disputes relating to the use and allocation of global resources.

The scope of that last phrase, "the use and allocation of global resources," can best be indicated by noting the kinds of problems with which I shall deal. They fall into two broad categories. The first category is treated in Part II under the heading "Sharing the Common Heritage." The situations discussed there concern such resource areas as ocean space, water basins and rivers, and, to some extent, the atmosphere and the general global environment. These areas give rise to the kind of problems associated with property or territorial rights, and involve such questions as access and transit, allocation of exploitation rights, the sharing of monopoly rents, responsibility for conservation, and liability for extraterritorial harm.

The second broad category, dealt with in Part III under the heading "Equity in Distribution," concerns problems of exchange and transfer of goods and services. Four major problems are examined: (1), the pricing and supply of basic raw materials; (2), the sharing of technology; (3), "sovereignty over natural resources"; and (4), world food security. Within these sections, consideration is given to proposals for more equitable distributive arrangements, as, for example, a "just" price for oil, limits on monopolistic or oligopolistic practices, commodity agreements, regulation of contracts for purchase of technology, control over transnational companies and foreign investment, and international food commitments and reserves. I realize that each of these subjects is in itself a large and complicated field of study on which a treatise can be written. But it is also possible—and I believe highly useful—to indicate briefly the significant new norms and procedures that are emerging in each of these areas and to consider their utility in meeting demands for equity and the other social ends sought by most governments.

Before dealing with these varied problems, however, I shall discuss the broad principles of entitlement which reflect the basic concepts of distributive justice as manifested in international decisions concerning resource allocation. My object is to clarify the value assumptions implicit in governmental positions and to point up the difficulties and dilemmas faced by collective bodies in seeking equity in the sharing of resources. This will be essentially an empirical analysis in the sense that it is based on the evaluative statements and behavior of governments and international organs rather than on theoretical assumptions. However, the record is complex and many-faceted. One must bear in mind that statements about equity and justice, especially those made by governments, often involve ambivalence and equivocation. When they are made in political bodies it is prudent to follow Wittgenstein's admonition, "don't look for the meaning, look for the use." After all, governments are not engaged in elaborating ideal systems but in coping with real grievances and conflicts. Yet we must also be careful not to wash away normative concepts and principles with an excessive dose of "cynical acid." They are part of the social reality: they shape the expectations and demands that give rise to conflict, and they help define the common basis for cooperative arrangements among states which have conflicting interests. That is why an examination of their meaning and use can have practical as well as intellectual significance, and it is especially with their practical significance in mind that I offer the following analysis. Perhaps "analysis" is not quite the right word; if I may borrow a phrase once again from Mr. Justice Holmes, my effort may be "more like painting a picture than doing a sum."

Equality and Need

Tocqueville's comments on the passion for equality, made more than a century ago, do not seem strange to observers of contemporary international assemblies. The political demands for more equitable distribution find much of their intellectual and emotive justification in the ideal of equality, and few question the high, and even primary, position of equality among social values. As one moves from the level of the ideal to practical social policy, however, it becomes apparent that equality is in itself too general a concept to support concrete policy choices. Choices must be made among the different kinds of equality: equality of rights, of opportunities, of conditions, and of outcome. And, these different kinds of equality may be incompatible in practice; indeed, this is likely to be the case when there are disparities in resources and capabilities. That is why, since the time of Plato it has been suggested that "equality among unequals" may be inequitable and that differential treatment may be essential for "real equality." We hear this reasoning echoed today in international bodies. However attractive the ideal of equality, governments (like social philosophers and jurists) are compelled to translate this ideal into specific valuational criteria if they are to resolve competing claims. In effect, then, general egalitarianism must become specific egalitarianism if it is to have practical application. That the selection of specific egalitarianism presents difficulties is readily indicated by the familiar conflicting standards for personal economic rewards—equal return for equal work, return based on productivity, or simply equal income (*tout court*), to which we must add equality of opportunity and of access, equality of property rights, and more. Nearly all of these kinds of equality among individuals have analogues in criteria which have been followed or proposed for relations among nations. As I see it, however, two basic criteria have particular importance in contemporary debates and decisions: one is a standard based on need, the other a standard based on legitimate expectation and historic entitlement. A consideration of these broad principles will throw light on the issues and dilemmas involved in applying the ideal of equity to the international division of the world's product.

I begin with the idea of entitlement based on need. This may seem, somewhat paradoxically, both obvious and utopian as a basis for international distribution. It has become virtually platitudinous to suggest that everyone is entitled to the necessities of life: food, shelter, health care, education, and the essential infrastructure for social organization. At the same time, it would be considered quixotic to suggest the classical Marxist maxim "to each according to his need" as a criterion of distribution. Even Marx regarded that principle as the distant goal of a classless and abundant society.[3] Yet when construed as a standard of minimal need it loses its utopian quality. Few today question the commitment of most states, capitalist and socialist, to meeting the minimal needs of their citizens. It is true that ideas of what minimal needs are vary with country and situation, but as a broad normative principle need is now so widely accepted in national societies as to be virtually beyond debate.

It is scarcely startling to find that a similar principle has been advanced on the international level. This does not lessen its importance. The fact that it has emerged as a widely accepted standard of international distribution has far-reaching practical implications. What is striking is not so much its espousal by the large majority of poor and handicapped countries but that the governments on the other side, to whom the demands for resources are addressed, have also by and large agreed that need is a legitimate and sufficient ground for preferential distribution. This agreement is evidenced not only by their concurrence in many international resolutions and by their own policy statements, but also, more convincingly, by a continuing series of actions to grant assistance and preferences to those countries in need. Though it may well be true that these actions fall short of meeting the actual requirements of many of the recipient countries, the scale and duration of the responses have been substantial enough to demonstrate the practical acceptance of the principle of need in contemporary international affairs.[4] It is true that the motivation of donor states will often include an element of self-interest (whether or not objectively well-founded), but this does not cancel out the significance of their response. Nor is its significance reduced by recognizing that state behavior reflects sociohistorical determinants, as Marxists and others suggest. Altruism is not necessary for an action to be equitable in its intent or effect.

It might be asked whether need has not always been an accepted standard for humanitarian assistance by nations as by individuals. It has, but there is an important difference between treating need as a matter of charity and linking it to the notion of justice. In the latter case, the satisfaction of needs is perceived as an entitlement, to be embodied in norms and institutions, and the relationship between donor and recipient is seen in terms of mutual rights and responsibilities.[5] On the other hand, when the provision of need is regarded as an act of charity, the relationship between the parties involved tends to be characterized by a sense of inequality, often with expectations of submissive behavior on the part of the recipient. Moreover, when viewed as charity, assistance is considered a matter of grace and is not readily institutionalized; deprivation is often regarded as an act of fate. Thus, the shift from a concept of charity to one of justice has had considerable importance for international actions and institutions, as shown by recent United Nations relief measures for countries severely affected by food deficits and the high price of essential imports. The shift has probably taken place because of the great increase in productivity and the expectations created by the new and potential patterns of distribution. In a world of meager resources, need was generally felt to be a natural calamity; it is only with the promise of global abundance, stimulated by new productive capability, that we find a widespread sense of injustice about the failure to meet needs. Clearly, this sense of injustice is no ephemeral phenomenon, nor is it one that can be attributed to transient political coalitions in international bodies. We must, I think, recognize it as a profound change in the perception of values, one with significant implications for international policy.

By treating need as a standard of equity (and of "real equality"), we reduce considerably the vagueness and indeterminacy of the concept of equitable sharing. Need, after all, can be ascertained in some objective way; there is even a widespread consensus on basic requirements of human beings everywhere. Still, defining needs on an international scale remains a complex, difficult task. It is not enough to distinguish needs from wants, as Aristotle did, though such differentiation remains a valid principle in the management of limited resources. Nor is it enough to calculate, as many have done, the essential needs of individual human beings for nutrition, health, shelter, education, security, and other factors. The more important and complicated issues involve the definition of needs in the light of social processes and their interaction. For example, in determining the food requirements of a country, one can begin with reasonably determinate facts such as nutritional requirements, population estimates, and available food supplies. But then to define needs in a prospective and operational sense, it is essential to consider the interrelation of several factors that determine supply and demand: the changing means of production, the input of capital and technology, the incentives to produce, the system of tenure and redistribution, the market and credit arrangements, prices, export demands, and several other conditioning elements. These factors are dynamic, and through their complex interactions the level of need for the people of a given region is determined. Obviously, then, the criterion of need does not provide simple answers even for a single problem such as food. It does, however, set a standard that can in principle be applied by objective factual inquiry.

Another type of problem faced in determining needs concerns the relation of collective needs to individual needs. Many have questioned the claims of developing countries which themselves have highly inequitable internal distribution of income. Gunnar Myrdal reports a typical question in donor countries: "Why do they not tax their own rich and reform their countries before they come to us with the begging bowl?" [6] Yet, valid as this question may be, it does not embrace the entire problem. When defining national needs, one must take into account the interaction between the needs of national states as collective entities and the needs of individual human beings. Even if one regards individual needs as the ultimate criterion (based on the premise that the state's only raison d'être is the well-being of its people), the requirements of a national state are relevant to certain public needs (for example, independence, security, growth) which are distinct from the distribution of economic benefits among its people. This distinction between national and personal needs does not mean that inequities within individual countries are of no international concern or that the sovereignty of a state precludes inquiry into such inequities by international bodies. But it does indicate that an international concept of need must take account of collective goods as well as of patterns of distribution.

Let me mention still another complex problem encountered when determining needs for purposes of equitable distribution. It concerns the need to allocate resources between present and future generations. The problem is not entirely a new one. Societies have always had to determine how much of their current consumption should be given up for investment and, therefore, for future generations. Economists see this as a problem of the optimum growth rate and mainly as a choice between private and social ends; that is, how much consumption should individuals be required to forego in order to maintain the economy or to meet other social needs, such as national security. When this is carried to great lengths (consider the Soviet Union's build-up of heavy industry and the consequent demands made on Soviet peoples), it is perceived by some as an issue of equity between present and future generations. In a more general way, some philosophers (for example, Herzen and Kant) have referred to the unfairness of earlier generations laboring for the benefit of later ones without reciprocity.[7] But this kind of inequity is accepted as part of the natural condition and only becomes a point of grievance where forced savings involve severe deprivation for contemporaries.

The issue of intergenerational equity has, however, taken a more acute turn because of the threatened environmental danger and resource depletion brought about by present rates of consumption. Even if the doomsday predictions of the "Limits to Growth" school are highly debatable, there is little doubt that the anticipated growth of population and industry will have serious consequences for future generations.[8] Increased awareness of these consequences means that the issue of the proper rate of growth will no longer be left to market forces or individual decisions. Making it a societal decision tends to bring out more sharply the problem of equity between generations and the extent of the sacrifice that should be made for the sake of posterity. In this context the distinction between needs and wants takes on new significance. We see it manifested in those movements which stress the wastefulness of consumption in affluent countries and those which warn of ecological dangers. The issue is further complicated by the apprehension that limiting economic growth in the interest of posterity will interfere with meeting the present needs of the poor. Formulas for selective growth and preferential distribution are responses to this problem which we shall consider later in more detail. At this point, I merely wish to point out the degree to which the issue of equitable sharing now tends toward a more objective standard of need in contrast to the economist's traditional standard of demand based on individual wants.

Although the issue of limited growth is usually discussed in terms of present versus future need, it is also valid to treat the needs of future generations as a part of present needs. After all, societies regard it as necessary to transmit to their descendents the social institutions and material base which they inherited and developed. That universally felt necessity is generally regarded as a justification for the renunciation of some present consumption through social saving and other transfers for the future. Seen in this way, the question of sacrificing for posterity becomes a matter of fulfilling actual needs of the present generation. It takes us from the much-debated but unanswerable question of reciprocity (what has posterity done for me?) to the determinate issue of how the needs of intergenerational transmission as perceived by specific societies should be satisfied in existing circumstances.

Finally, there is the conception of global needs as distinct from national needs and from an aggregation of individual needs. The recent concern with this dimension of needs had been greatly stimulated by three interrelated attitudes: (1), the apprehension over ecological and resource depletion; (2), the awareness of linkages and mutual interactions, summed up by the term "global interdependence"; (3), the interest in systems theory and systems approaches as methodologies for dealing with international problems. The fashionable metaphor of the "spaceship earth" and the concepts of "interdependence," "integrative planning," and "total designs" all figure prominently in the discussion of global needs. Under the influence of natural science systems models, some theorists emphasize the requisites for the "global system" to maintain its equilibrium and to adapt itself to internal and external influences.[9] This emphasis often tends toward formalistic taxonomy, especially when human beings and their aspirations are treated as "black-box" units (i.e., their contents are ignored). But my reservations about some systems theories do not mean that I reject the relevance of global needs. I am only dubious about formalistic approaches which rely too heavily on physical and biological models and exclude actual human goals and sociohistorical factors. I think it necessary to give concrete meaning to the concept of global needs, and I should like to mention three approaches to that task.

The first approach is to look to the physical and technological areas which transcend national boundaries. The obvious subjects of current concern are the oceans, the atmosphere, the overall climate; in these areas, needs such as the conservation of resources and protection against dangers to human health and to other species are now identified on a global level. Methods of global monitoring, such as "earthwatch" and the "integrated global ocean station system," are being instituted to determine the specific character of those needs. Meeting them would clearly come within a general policy of equitable sharing, even though such a policy served collective requirements rather than preferential distribution.

A somewhat different approach to the definition of global needs derives from the worldwide character of certain patterns of interaction. Perhaps the best-known example of this is the food-population-resource equation, which is an oversimplified way of referring to a series of interrelated problems that have to be dealt with in terms of global quantities and effects. Another example is suggested by the "international development strategy" adopted by the United Nations in an effort to bring into a coherent relationship the many interactive elements that affect development on a worldwide basis. Both of these examples indicate that in order to define global needs, one must go beyond aggregating separate national requirements.[10] The methodology and empirical data now available are still not adequate, however, and much remains to be done if the generalities about interdependence are to be transformed into reasonably specific conclusions that are usable for policy decisions. It also remains to be seen whether or not governments which are almost entirely concerned with their own national requirements will encourage efforts to identify global needs as an independent category.

The third approach to worldwide needs is rather more political and less technocratic than the two others just described. It focuses on the conception of a world economy composed of three sectors: a core of advanced industrial states, a semiperiphery of socialist countries, and a periphery of underdeveloped countries which are mainly sources of raw materials.[11] The features stressed in this conception are the hegemonic role of the core countries and the inferior position of the periphery. When viewed from this third perspective (which has been advanced by some spokesmen from the Third World), the most critical global need is the elimination of the stratification and the relation of dominance and subordination in the world economy. Although explicitly directed against the core states, this approach claims support based on the universal values of equity and justice. Thus, in a way, it brings us around full circle to our quest for the meaning of real equality and equitable sharing of the world's product.

It is evident from our discussion that in seeking to relate equitable sharing to ascertainable needs, we encounter a number of complex problems. Some of them are difficult to solve because of intellectual limitations; we have insufficient knowledge of causal relations and not enough factual data. Others involve what we may describe as political difficulties; they require choices which will mean sacrifices and high costs for some. Later we shall consider some of the institutional structures and arrangements which have been suggested or employed to deal with these problems. However, these various difficulties do not mean that the criterion of need is chimerical as a standard of equitable distribution. As we shall see in more detail, many international decisions affecting the allocation and distribution of resources seek to meet specific needs on a preferential basis. Of course, the world is still very far from accepting the utopian goal of "to each according to his need" even in theory, but it is undeniable that the fulfillment of the needs of the poor and disadvantaged countries has been recognized as a normative principle which is central to the idea of equity and distributive justice. That this principle has been given a measure of practical effect in collective decisions is attributable, I believe, not to a sudden spread of altruism, but to a widely felt necessity on the part of governmental elites to respond to tensions and grievances which threaten the equilibrium and stability of the international order. The implications of this new response for the norms and structures of the international system are only just beginning to be examined.

Legitimate Expectations and Historic Entitlement

Although in international bodies equity has been increasingly identified with meeting the needs of the disadvantaged, other notions of fairness and justice are also evidenced in regard to the distribution of resources. The most significant of these has an affinity to the idea of proportionate equality as used by Aristotle: that equality should be proportionate to what is due or deserved.[12] Initially this idea appears to be little more than a tautology—"to each his due"—but it leads us to consider the basis of entitlement and the legitimate expectations which flow from it. In national societies such expectations usually derive from social norms and institutions, and this would seem to be true on the international level also. Principles of legitimacy and control, norms governing trade and exchange, and an extensive array of accepted practice relating to distribution all create the expectations that enable participants to recognize what is due and deserved.

You will note that these expectations are not usually based on any general valuational principle (such as need, or merit, or efficiency), nor are they dependent on a desired pattern of results. They are generated by the processes of acquisition and transfer, whether the results are considered good or bad. We need only remind ourselves that the great bulk of the world's resources has been divided among numerous sovereignties by a historic process, and that our conception of entitlement to those resources is largely determined by the legitimacy accorded that process. When governments insist on their sovereign authority over their own natural resources and their rights to use and dispose of these resources freely (to determine who may exploit and purchase and at what price and conditions), they are basing their position on the legitimacy of their acquisition and on what they deem to be their just due. We can observe this in the disputes of governments with foreign enterprises, in their claims to adjacent ocean space, in their control over exports and access to their markets, and in various other manifestations of territorial jurisdiction. Their ideas of what is just and fair in their international relations are profoundly influenced by their conception of their sovereign rights. Nor is this influence limited to territorial sovereignty. Just entitlement may also include access to and use of natural resources outside of national jurisdiction, as, for example, historic fishery rights or customary transit rights over land or waters. Efforts to reduce or eliminate such acquired rights run counter to concepts of fairness and justice.[13] The same holds true for entitlements arising from international agreements and the norms governing consensual transactions. These not only create expectations as to future behavior; they also condition attitudes about the equities involved. Holmes's "bad man" theory of contract does not quite fit international dealings; when states enter into treaties they are not simply buying an option to perform or pay damages. The commitment is itself a determinant of what is due and therefore of what is equitable, irrespective of the merits of the transaction. Of course there are exceptions, but we need not have a categorical rule to substantiate our conclusion about the general bearing of entitlement on ideas of equity.

In the light of these observations it may seem strange that in current discussions equity and distributive justice are identified almost entirely with the demands of the poor and disadvantaged for a larger share of resources, and that they are rarely used to refer to the kind of entitlements I have described. Perhaps one reason for this situation is that economists tend to employ the term equity (or distributive justice) as virtually a code word for wider income distribution and transfer payments to the poor. But this special meaning overlooks the significance of entitlements in actual disputes between nations in which strong feelings of injustice have been generated. Consider, for example, the dispute between Iceland and the United Kingdom over Iceland's claim to an extended, exclusive fishing zone, which came before the International Court of Justice in 1974; or the more general class of disputes between capital-exporting states and host countries over nationalization and contractual rights pertaining to foreign investment in natural resources; or the claims of lower riparians to a share of clean river water (as in the dispute between Mexico and the United States over the salination of the Colorado River).[14] In these resource disputes, the equities asserted have been based on each side's conception of what was due to it and that, in turn, rested on historic and consensual processes and norms derived from them. Clearly, the idea of equity has a much wider meaning for governments than it does for economists and others who use it to refer to increasing the share of those less well-off. Nor should this be surprising. After all, the world's resources are distributed in accordance with entitlements based on territorial rights, custom, and consensual transactions, and it is only natural that ideas of equity should be significantly determined by that reality.

But how, it may be asked, can this idea be reconciled with the concept of equity as meeting the needs of the poor and disadvantaged? One way, evidenced in international debate, is to link demands based on needs to entitlements derived from accepted principles. For example, the claims of landlocked states and new states for access to and sharing of ocean resources have been advanced not so much on the basis of needs as on the basis that such access is due these states under the principle of the common heritage (the *res communis*) of the oceans. Similarly, in river disputes lower riparian countries assert not only their need for adequate supplies of water but also a customary or treaty right and on the latter basis may demand changes in the pattern of use and appropriation by the upper riparians. Even the broad and generalized demands of poor countries for preferences and grants are often advanced as entitlements owed to them because of past exploitation, oligopolistic restraints, or other allegedly illegitimate practices of the industrialized societies. Such demands illustrate a general tendency to utilize the two conceptions of equity in harness as mutually supportive rather than antagonistic principles of valuation. This is not merely a matter of "dialectics" or rhetoric. It reflects a political judgment that as an international criterion the maxim "to each according to his need" is too impractical and far-reaching in its implications to win acceptance as a general principle; but that when this maxim is conjoined with and limited by a principle of legitimacy, it becomes more acceptable because less threatening to the international order. In short, the Aristotelian principle of distributive justice may be seen as implicit in the normative assumptions of governments and as providing a counterpoint to competing egalitarian conceptions.

The interplay and linkage of the competing conceptions of equity are evidenced in two international principles which have received wide support in recent years. One is the principle of permanent sovereignty over natural resources. The other is the principle of rectification of past injustices. Later we shall have occasion to learn how both of these ideas have played roles in specific controversies over the distribution of resources. At this point, I should like only to indicate briefly how they are related to the two criteria of equity we have been discussing.

"Permanent sovereignty over natural resources" is linked to what I have called historic entitlement. Its normative premise is that territorial jurisdiction resulting from a historic process of acquisition is the paramount basis for rights over natural resources and that, in consequence, it is just and equitable to recognize the ascendancy of that principle in international decisions pertaining to resources. Each

sovereignty has its "proportionate equality," however unequal its actual share may be. At the same time, the concept
of permanent sovereignty is perceived by the less-developed
countries as a defense against alleged exploitation by the
more advanced countries and their enterprises. They use it
primarily to obtain a greater share for themselves, and it is
therefore asserted to justify nationalization and other take-
over measures directed against foreign enterprises, to limit
profits and their repatriation, to remove foreign restraints
on the transfer of technology, to override contractual arrangements on the grounds of public interest and need,
and so on. Significantly, "permanent sovereignty" is rarely,
if ever, advanced as an entitlement of the affluent countries
in their relations with the less-developed countries. Thus,
decisions by the richer countries to restrict exports or to impose restraints on access to their markets are not justified by
international bodies as proper exercises of "sovereignty
over resources" but are regarded often as undesirable and
unfair actions against the poorer countries. From one perspective this difference in attitude can be criticized as a double standard of sovereign rights, yet from another it may be
seen as an indication of a single standard, namely, the principle of meeting the needs of the disadvantaged. We thus
find in the concept of permanent sovereignity over resources a principle which is, so to speak, conservative in its
stress on sovereign rights (based on historic acquisition) yet
utilized by poor countries as a weapon of change.

In a somewhat analogous way, the idea of rectification
of past wrongs has been advanced primarily as a right of
disadvantaged countries with, again, the implication of a
double standard in its application to developed and developing states. There is, of course, nothing new in the demand of governments and peoples for correction of historic
injustices. In a sense that demand is the other side of the
coin of historic entitlement. If entitlements are based on the

legitimacy of the process of acquisition, they should also be open to attack on grounds of their illegitimacy and injustice; acts of fraud or the illegal use of force would vitiate an entitlement for reasons of equity, if not in law.[15] We find this general notion of rectification reflected also in claims of unjust enrichment, advanced, for example, by governments which claim compensation for inordinate profits said to have been made by foreign concessions under conditions of political or economic domination. Even though such claims have received little support in judicial cases, they have been expressed in political bodies and in declarations of principle adopted in organs of the United Nations. For example, in 1974 the General Assembly declared that states and peoples which have been under "foreign occupation, alien and colonial domination" have the right to restitution and full compensation "for the exploitation and depletion of, and damages to, the natural and all other resources." [16] One cannot but be struck by the breadth of this asserted principle when one thinks of the numerous countries in the developed areas of the world as well as in the Third World which have suffered even in the recent past from alien domination and foreign occupation. Almost certainly the proponents of the UN declaration had the poor countries primarily in mind as its beneficiaries, but the declaration's sweeping language and the grievances felt in many developed countries about foreign domination may presage its political use outside of the Third World. But even if the declaration is limited to the claims of developing countries, its scope is so wide and its meaning so uncertain as to cast doubt on the feasibility of its practical implementation.

These intrinsic difficulties do not mean that the notion of rectification will be ignored. It is too firmly grounded in widely held conceptions of justice to disappear from political and juridical claims. More specifically, it is a consequence of accepting entitlements based on the process of acquisition rather than on end-results, for, as we noted, if there are historic rights, there will inevitably be historic wrongs. One could say that the principle of rectification is the natural and radical offspring of the conservative concept of acquired rights. Just how far this principle will be carried in international affairs and in what specific forms remain to be seen, but it seems likely that it will be utilized as still another conceptual weapon by dissatisfied governments seeking to change existing patterns of distribution.

My observations on the role of entitlements and need have, I hope, clarified my earlier reference to the dialectical interplay of competing notions of equity. I have sought to show how these two opposing criteria of distributive justice have been applied as mutually supportive grounds for new principles of equity asserted in international bodies and indeed how difficult it would be, in a political sense, to apply either one without the other. This analysis, as I have said, is essentially empirical; it is not based on moral theory or philosophical premises but rather on the actual positions taken by governments in their claims and responses regarding the world's resources. These positions are a product of existing tensions and conflicts. They are not ideal constructions, and they naturally manifest ambivalences and indeterminacies. But, as I have tried to show, they also reveal certain basic normative concepts which influence evaluative behavior and which give some determinate meaning and political force to the ideal of distributive justice.

Competing Goals and Collective Decisions

Of course, equity is not the only social value sought in international arenas. Even the institutions which frequently receive and respond to demands for distributive justice (such as UNCTAD) are not specialized structures for dealing with such issues. In fact, their terms of reference are explicitly directed toward other objectives—trade, development, coordination of national effort, integration—so that issues of equitable treatment usually arise in the context of a wider range of goals and criteria. Nor are the stated aims of such international bodies the only aims that matter; the participants always pursue other goals. National security, independence, and prestige may be more important to many of them than either equity or economic efficiency. It is also evident that the multiple goals and the efforts to pursue them are frequently in conflict with each other, and the concrete problem is often one of achieving a proper balance or trade-off among competing values.

The idea of trade-offs is especially prominent when issues of equity are in the forefront. In economic matters, this is linked to the widely held belief that greater equality and wider sharing are likely to be antithetical to the goals of efficiency and productivity. Stated in the language of utilitarian economics, "the sum of utilities would be considerably smaller at complete equality (and near-complete equality) than under redistributive programs allowing significantly more incentive for differentials in retained disposable income and utility." [17] Although this proposition and its variants have been subjected to much refined economic analysis (which has produced certain qualifications), it still expresses a major international and national policy-making dilemma that is relevant to both the allocation and the use of resources. We may observe parenthetically that this dilemma holds for the socialist centrally planned economies as well as for market economies, and for the industrialized as well as for the developing countries. As long as resources are scarce, there will be a problem of relating differentials in income distribution to the requirements of production and efficient use of the resource endowment of national states. The problem is also present (although in somewhat different aspects) in most of the principal international issues relating to the distribution and use of resources. It is manifested or implicit in the debates on international transfer payments, commodity pricing and stabilization, the transfer of technology, the control of multinational companies, the management of seabed resources, fishing rights, the system of food reserves, even in debates on outer space. On the whole, it is reasonably clear to those who are concerned that in these matters claims of equity and wider sharing may have negative effects on other values, particularly on economic productivity and, in some situations, on national autonomy. That a trade-off and balance must be sought is an obvious conclusion.

However, this conclusion leads us to the complexities of international decision making. We must remember that a trade-off among competing values is one thing for a single decision maker and quite another for a collective body. The single decision maker (whether it be an individual or a national authority) can determine its own ranking order for the relevant values and, taking that order into account, can seek to maximize its net value position. In doing so it will strike a compromise among the competing goals of efficiency, autonomy, stability, equity, and so on. In a collective body, however, the existence of divergent individual ranking of ends requires, if decisions are to be taken, a "master" ordering of values that necessarily differs from one or more of the individual orderings. (If it did not, the individual orderings would not be divergent, and if unanimity existed, there would be no problem of choice.) In this sense a master ordering implies an imposed decision; no voting arrangement, however democratic, can avoid such an imposition as long as the individual constituent parties maintain their divergent positions. This truth has been demonstrated in elegant abstract postulational analysis by Kenneth Arrow [18] (and refined and argued over by others), but the basic point is obvious enough in international arenas where participant countries are acutely conscious of their autonomy and sovereignty. The problems of achieving a consensus (or, in the older language, ascertaining the general will) have not escaped the diplomats. They are fully aware (though the point is rarely made explicit) that a genuine consensus on the ranking of social ends is almost impossible to attain in a heterogeneous body of nation-states with different interests and social systems.

This difficulty is especially evident when the issues among countries involve claims of equity as against claims of productivity, national autonomy, or stability. That does not mean that the issues are laid aside or that the demands for justice disappear. Solutions are sought on various levels of international activity. These levels fall, broadly speaking, into two categories: one, bargaining; the other, institutional procedures. Bargaining remains the characteristic and, some might say, the natural modality for striking a balance among competing interests and thus, to a certain extent, among conflicting values. This is so whether transactions are conducted in a free market or under regulated conditions. The recent intensification of demands for distributive justice has not only introduced new elements into international bargaining but has also produced greater concern about the conditions of bargaining on the multilateral level. Such concern is manifested in proposals and arrangements for facilitating the bargaining process and rendering it more equitable. An important aspect relates to improving the "transparency" of international economic dealings by providing a much greater flow of reliable information about the factors affecting demand and supply. Proposals range from an ambitious plan for a global intelligence system that would monitor information regarding resources and prices to more limited measures such as increasing the exchange of information on demand and supply factors for specific commodities or reporting on activities of transnational companies. Although these informational proposals may be justified as facilitating bargaining under market conditions, they are far from noncontroversial. Yet, as we shall see, many of the new schemes affecting resource distribution are premised on mechanisms for greater transparency in sensitive economic matters.

Procedural measures for improved bargaining are also directed toward improving the conditions of negotiation and consultation among the parties to the bargaining process. An important and controversial aspect concerns the relation of producers' associations to collective bodies for the consuming and importing countries. The need for appropriate bargaining between these two sides has produced a variety of proposals on the procedures and modalities of such collective negotiation.[19] Stress also has been placed on the need for consultative procedures in cases affecting resource distribution and use. Proposals to require consultation have been warmly debated in international bodies over a wide range of issues including, for example, environmental damage, the use of water resources, earth satellite sensing, oceanographic research, and commodity pricing. Despite the difficulties of and resistance to such requirements, one can discern a trend toward greater acceptability of consultative procedures in regard to national actions affecting the resources of other countries.[20] There is also increased interest in the exclusion of practices which interfere with good faith negotiation and consultation. The most important, as well as the most debated, issue in this respect concerns restrictions on the use of economic coercion. Of special concern is the use of economic coercion to achieve objectives of a political or strategic kind or to interfere with a state's authority over its own domestic affairs.[21] We can also foresee an interest in rules and procedures that would protect the collective responsibility of negotiating groups against actions, such as bilateral deals, which would make collective bargaining impossible. Finally, there is an interest in promoting conditions for the more reliable fulfillment of expectations, particularly in assuring security of supply and markets, in stabilizing price relationships, and in avoiding disruptive behavior. The mere recital of these problems and objectives is sufficient to delineate the kind of procedural law and "rules of the game" that will be needed to produce conditions of fair bargaining and, in that respect, to facilitate rational choices among competing interests and goals.

Although no sharp line can be drawn between bargaining and institutional procedures (since the latter normally reflect negotiations among the parties concerned), the decisions of international bodies often go beyond bargaining in affecting or determining collective choices among conflicting objectives. Such institutional decisions can be seen as taking place on three levels. The first level is that of general principles and aims typically expressed in resolutions adopted by quasi-parliamentary organs of global scope such as the General Assembly and UNCTAD. Two types of such normative resolutions can be distinguished. One is the classic "balanced" resolution which seeks to accommodate all important interests and thus obtain universal support. Balanced resolutions express diverse and competing aims without laying down a hierarchy of values or a criteria of choice between antithetical objectives. The other type of resolution is the more one-sided, equity-oriented resolution which articulates the intensely felt demands of the majority political coalition for a wider distribution of resources. This type of resolution, now more prevalent than the former in United Nations bodies, lacks a genuine worldwide consensus (though sometimes adopted by a technical "consensus" procedure in order to avoid voting) and is regarded by many of the more affluent states as unbalanced.[22] Obviously, resolutions of this second type do not seek to present a paradigm of rational choice but rather to further a specific type of change. By expressing majority demands as principles and obligations (moral, if not legal), they aim both at delegitimizing norms which were previously influential and engendering expectations as to future patterns of more equitable distribution. Whether or not they are likely to have that effect, in the absence of a genuine consensus of all concerned, has been argued about, especially in the rich countries, but it seems hard to deny that there has been a significant shift in attitudes and expectations in line with the principles of these resolutions. Our earlier discussion of the importance now given to meeting basic needs of the less well-off and disadvantaged countries has already made that point. One need not attribute to resolutions of international bodies a decisive role in bringing about that shift in expectations in order to recognize that they have an influential and probably unique role in that respect.

Although resolutions of the kind just discussed have been in the forefront of discussion, they constitute only a small segment of the institutional decisions concerned with the sharing of resources. Many other decisions are made on a more specific plane by the various international organs composed of territorial or functional groupings, as in fisheries and river basin commissions, commodity bodies, producers' associations, Common Market arrangements, and a variety of other multinational economic institutions. On the whole these bodies, with their limited membership and specialized responsibilities, can more readily achieve consensus than can the heterogeneous global organs. Moreover, the criteria they lay down or apply, whether in the form of rules or policy decisions, are generally complied with, whatever their formal legal character.[23] Their decisions do, of course, involve bargaining, but that bargaining is substantially affected by the institutional context in which it occurs. Obvious examples of this are the influence of international secretariats and of political coalitions as well as the aims and limits imposed by the basic constituent agreement.

As might be expected, these specialized organs, in contrast to the more heterogeneous global bodies, do not address themselves to the larger issues of global reform or rectification of past injustices. Yet they almost always have to be mindful of equity in the sharing of benefits among their parties. Otherwise the essentially voluntary arrangements for cooperation would cease to be viable, and they would either collapse or possibly be transformed into more dictatorial or hegemonial structures. Consequently, issues of equitable treatment among the parties, in respect to both losses and gains, are often critical to the functioning of these bodies and of great concern when their constitutional foundations are laid. In many cases, the only acceptable safeguard for states with substantial resources at stake is a firm requirement of unanimity (or "consensus") for decisions of any importance. In a few situations, more complex voting procedures for qualified majority decisions and constitutional provisions to protect minority rights have been adopted.[24] Agreement on substantive criteria for equitable distribution may, in some cases, be a condition precedent for the acceptance of a rule-making or allocating organ as we have seen in riparian and fishing commissions or in the new International Energy Authority.

There is still a third level of institutional decisions affecting resource allocation: the level of operational or executive action. Included in this composite category are the acts of international financial agencies in transferring capital, the technical assistance and informational activities of many of the United Nations agencies and of various regional bodies, and even the occasional managerial functions of international bodies directly responsible for resource management (as, for example, in buffer stock operations, or in the embryonic seabed authority). Although all such operational activities take place within a framework of governing rules and precepts, the concrete executive decisions still require choices and trade-offs among conflicting ends. A history of policy trends in the World Bank or of the controversies in the United Nations Development Programme reveal the extent to which demands for greater efficiency, for more national autonomy, and for equity (seen in terms of needs and entitlement) have competed with each other in operational decisions and have required a series of accommodations by the international organs.[25] We note this not to assert that the accommodations reached were satisfactory, but to underline the continuing, almost day-to-day, process of collective international bargaining to reach decisions involving competing social ends.

Clearly such collective determinations cannot always conform to the divergent value rankings of the different states concerned, and in that strict sense, they are imposed decisions. The political implications are manifested in the tendencies of governments to limit such operational agencies and to require the specific agreement of host states to any activities on their territory. Questions concerning the distribution of power and authority for collective decisions generally result in conflicting positions taken by major groups, depending on how these groups perceive their chances of exerting influence and avoiding decisions against their interest. This state of affairs is especially evident when new institutions are being established. The same constitutional issues arise time and again. Should the terms of the constituent agreement be drafted tightly, with detailed prescriptions for operations? How should the intergovernmental governing bodies be composed to give appropriate representation or parity to competing blocs? Should their decisions be taken by general agreement, by special majorities (as in weighted voting), or by a simple majority? To what extent should the executive staff be politically representative of governments and how should their discretionary authority be controlled? These and related questions have become perennial issues in international organization; they are especially contentious when the institutions involved are operational and their decisions managerial rather than advisory. It is true that precedents and patterns have been established, but they are continually being challenged as political coalitions develop and new demands arise. The controversy over the regime for the seabed is a good illustration, as we shall see later. What is evident is that the procedures for international decision making cannot be determined by some ideal model. They have to be seen as problems in the distribution of power to be solved through political processes which take account of relative national capabilities and needs as well as the shared interest in cooperation.

This does not mean that there is no room for rules and standards to promote rational and equitable decision making. Just as bargaining among states may be placed on a firmer basis by suitable rules of the game (as I suggested above), so the institutional arrangements concerned with multinational resource-sharing problems may benefit from similar measures to improve the rationality and fairness of collective decisions. For example, practical steps leading to the greater transparency of world economic activities and to early consultation on the transnational effects of domestic actions would strengthen many of the regulatory and operational institutions. Nor is it unrealistic to seek the acceptance of standards of behavior which would facilitate collective decisions and avoid unilateral or group action disruptive to cooperative arrangements. Some examples of this may be found in some of the specialized regional schemes that relate to trade and resource management. What is needed, one might optimistically suggest, is a kind of "constitutional law" which would prescribe broad principles of reasonable behavior relevant to international cooperation and which would be applicable to all the diverse economic bodies. We are still far from such law but some of the new proposals for sharing resources and wealth point in that direction.

One should not expect that any such emergent constitutional precepts would prescribe a master order of values for all situations. In our pluralistic and heterogeneous world such a master order would be neither sensible nor feasible. What we might reasonably expect and seek to promote is a more sustained effort to identify and clarify the multiple goals shared by most peoples and to relate these goals to specific situations and proposed actions. In that effort, the goal of international equity with which we have been primarily concerned may become more precise and also seen in a wider context than it previously has been. A process of concretization should occur so that diverse situations may be distinguished for purposes of ordering priorities and goals. We can already see this in the special categories emerging for international preferences—the desperately needy Fourth World, the underdeveloped but financially prosperous oil producers, the landlocked countries, the desert areas, the resource-poor industrialized countries, those threatened by environmental damage, and so on. The main components of international equity that we have discussed above—the satisfaction of basic needs, the respect for entitlement and legitimate expectation, the ideal of equality—must be applied to these special categories and to other diverse factual situations in ways appropriate to their particular characteristics. The conceptions of distributive justice provide standards and a sense of direction; they do not prescribe specific solutions.

Moreover, as we saw, in actual situations legitimate demands for equity must be linked to the other major goals of states and peoples. When resources are scarce, their equitable sharing cannot be isolated from the consideration of productive capacity and the means of increasing supply. Nor can the measures for more equitable treatment be pursued without regard to the intense demands for independence and autonomy which may be antithetical to goals of sharing and production. We cannot, in short, escape from the reality of pluralist goals and the necessities of trade-offs and compromise. But the effort to clarify our values—to analyze their complex and ambivalent meanings—and to relate them to specific circumstances can enable us to see the problems in the round, to detect our intellectual and factual deficiencies, and to identify more precisely the sacrifices and the benefits that may result. These become highly practical objectives at a time when governments are groping uncertainly toward new international structures to meet the grievances and anxieties of a troubled world.

Part II
Sharing the Common Heritage

NOT surprisingly, problems of equitable sharing have arisen most directly over parts of the globe where resources are shared by more than one country. The oceans, the most important of these areas, are currently the setting for competing claims of equity that have produced a series of conflicts and new conceptions of entitlement which are profoundly altering the regime of the seas. Another significant category comprises the international waterways, lakes, and water basins shared by two or more countries. Here too we can see how rising demands and real or threatened water scarcity are shaping ideas of equitable appropriation and leading to new arrangements for sharing. A third category, one that is just beginning to be viewed as shared property, is the atmosphere or, more broadly, the global environment. Although the notion of equitable sharing of the atmosphere is still in embryonic form, the potential disputes relating to weather modification and the foreseeable threats of damage presage the development of new law. Diverse as they are, all three categories can be regarded in a broad sense as governed by a general principle of equitable use and appropriation. In the discussion that follows, I shall indicate how this principle is being given specific content under the pressures of technological development, increased demands, and the broad movement for a wider distribution of wealth.

Sharing and Exclusivity
in the Oceans

It may seem paradoxical that a movement begun in the United Nations to achieve an equitable sharing of the newly found wealth of the oceans should have resulted in the vast extension of exclusive resource zones under national jurisdiction. That this has occurred has been attributed to the strong nationalist tendencies in the developing world and to the diminished power of the large maritime nations. It has also been seen as a response to demands for greater equity and wider sharing. One is bound to ask why the principle of *res communis* for the oceans—so long enshrined in international law—should now have been attacked as inequitable and greatly reduced in its application. What could be more equitable than a principle which guarantees access to all on an equal basis and excludes appropriation by anyone?

In reflecting on this question, it may be helpful to consider the oceans as a collective good (or public good) in the specific sense in which that term is used by economists and political scientists.[1] Two rather different examples of a collective good are the public parks and the system of public health. They each exhibit certain attributes essential to the definition of a collective good. One is that the benefits of a user do not diminish another's benefits (in that sense, they are "jointly available goods"). A second is that their use and enjoyment cannot be divided up for individual benefits; in effect, the collective good is indivisible. Two other attributes may be said to follow from the first two: a collective good is nonappropriable and freely accessible to all. It is easy to see that free access to all and nonappropriability will be regarded as equitable because the first two conditions exist—that is, use by one does not reduce the benefits to others and the benefits cannot be divided up among users. From the standpoint of equity it has little significance that some use and enjoy the park more than others.

Are the oceans a collective good in the same way as the public parks? Until recently, they were thought to be. It was generally assumed that with respect to the main benefits of the oceans—fishing and navigation—the oceans were indivisible and the benefits jointly available. In Grotius's words, "The sea, since it is as incapable of being seized as the air, cannot be attached to the possessions of any particular nation." There was, moreover, enough ocean for all. Under these conditions, enjoyment by some could not reduce the benefits, actual or potential, for others. Free access for all and a prohibition against appropriation could not but appear as unqualifiedly equitable.

In recent years, however, it has become evident that the conditions of joint availability and indivisibility are no longer applicable to the removable resources of the ocean. The fish, once seemingly unlimited in quantity, are not enough for all; harvesting by one will often reduce the catch of others. The new resources, oil, gas, and hard minerals, are also not "jointly available." For it cannot be said that their exploitation would not diminish the availability of the resource to others. Nor can it be said that the exploitation of these removable resources is indivisible. They can, in most cases, be divided up, though as we shall see below, there are limitations of some significance in allocating fisheries.

In sum, the criteria of a collective good no longer apply to the removable resources of the ocean, although they still hold for navigation and communication. The important consequence of this change is that freedom of access and nonappropriability are no longer regarded as "natural" conditions or as equitable. They are, in fact, perceived as inequitable because free access and exploitation have often redounded to the benefit of the richer and stronger countries, irrespective of relative needs for the resource or geographical relationships. Moreover, unrestricted access, especially when supported by new technological means, has led to overexploitation and economic waste, most clearly evident in respect to fishing. We can see why the countries which felt injured by a regime of free access have moved to change that system. They have sought to replace it in part with a regime of national property rights for coastal states (the "exclusive economic zones") and in part by an international managerial regime for the seabed beyond national jurisdiction. At the same time they have agreed to maintain the traditional freedoms of navigation and communication. These three features, it now seems clear, will be the principal components of the new law of the sea that will be formulated in the treaty likely to be concluded in 1978. Only one of these components—the freedom of navigation and communication—expresses the Grotian conception of *res communis.* The other two involve substantial departures from the traditional principles of freedom of the seas and unrestricted access to its benefits. They represent, albeit in quite different ways, the felt necessity for regulation of marine resource exploitation. They also reflect in some respects the conceptions of equity discussed in Part I as well as factors of national interest and power. We can see how these elements are related to each other by looking at the evolution of the system of exclusive economic zones and the way in which it has sought to accommodate competing interests and claims.

Long before the conclusion of the prolonged Third Conference on the Law of the Sea, it became apparent that coastal states would obtain the right to exercise jurisdiction over the living and nonliving resources within the 200-mile zones beyond their shorelines.* This was welcomed by many of the developing countries as a major step toward the wider sharing of ocean resources and as a victory over the affluent countries which had profited from a regime of open seas. There is an element of irony in the fact that the process which led to this result began with the action of the United States in the Truman Declaration of 1945 unilaterally extending its jurisdiction over the resources of the continental shelf beyond the territorial sea. This unilateral

---

* This will almost surely result from state practice accepted as law, even if the treaty has not been concluded or come into force.

measure rather quickly became accepted as customary law and was then codified in the 1958 Geneva Convention on the Continental Shelf. The rapid development of technology for the extraction of offshore petroleum and natural gas and the rising demands for energy made it plain to coastal states that the extension of national jurisdiction over shelf resources could be of immese economic value, and in many cases it has proved to be so.[2] While the precise limitation of the zone of exclusive jurisdiction over the marginal seabed was not easily agreed upon, the basic nationalist trend was reflected in the wide support for extending the shelf to the outer edge of the continental margin, regardless of distance.[3]

One could not be surprised that a similar extension over the superjacent waters was soon claimed by coastal states that were either dependent on fishing in adjacent waters or sensitive to the exploitation of those waters by distant-water fishing fleets of other countries. A critical factor was that the long-held assumption of unlimited harvest from the seas could no longer be maintained; overfishing and depletion were evident in many areas. This coincided with a considerable increase in the demand for fish due to population growth, higher incomes, and new uses for fish products (as for animal feed). The imbalance between supply and demand was compounded by the improved technology which vastly increased the catch and often brought fish levels below biological reproduction standards. The consequence, as summarized by a leading economist in this field, was that "The international fisheries move steadily toward an organizational structure that yields rising prices and has more and more labour and capital pursuing the same number or fewer fish. At the very least this is a formula for economic failure." [4] It was also a formula for vigorous national protectionism by coastal states which, in hardly more than two decades, succeeded in overturning much of the traditional system of open access to fisheries against the solid opposition of the most powerful maritime countries in the world.

It is interesting to observe how this process was reflected in three successive juridical conceptions. First came the acceptance of the principle that the coastal states have a natural interest in, and therefore a special right to protect, fish stocks in areas of the high seas adjacent to their territorial seas. This legal principle can be seen in its embryonic form in the International Court of Justice judgment in the Anglo-Norwegian Fisheries Case of 1951.[5] It was more clearly stated in a resolution of the 1958 Geneva Conference on the Law of the Sea, then followed by state practice which was given judicial recognition in the International Court's judgment of 1974 in the fisheries case involving Iceland and the United Kingdom.[6] The principle of special protection then evolved into the concept of preferential rights for coastal states, especially in favor of countries which were highly dependent on fishing in adjacent waters. That principle was supported by a large majority in the Geneva Conferences of 1958 and 1960 (though not included in any Geneva treaty), and it was subsequently given effect in various bilateral and multinational agreements.[7] The International Court placed its judicial imprimatur on the concept in the 1974 Iceland-United Kingdom fisheries case.

The third step in this judicial progression was the movement from preference to exclusive jurisdiction. This was marked by a series of forcible actions by some coastal states against distant-water fishing fleets. (The seizures by Equador and Peru of American tuna-fishing boats and the cod-fishing "war" of Iceland against the British were notable examples.) As the Third Law of the Sea Conference went through its several stages, the concept of the 200-mile exclusive economic zone received increasing support though differences remained as to the obligations and international accountability of the coastal states (to which I shall refer later). In the end the powerful and wealthy countries, which were originally opposed to the exclusive economic zone, supported it. This apparent victory of the many small countries over the few powerful countries has been hailed (or deplored) as evidence of the increased influence of "democratized" international lawmaking when the majority has the ability to maintain an effective political coalition. It has also been stressed as significant that the major powers found themselves unable to employ armed force effectively to protect what they considered to be their lawful rights in the waters claimed by the coastal states. The intensified nationalism characteristic of nearly all of the developing countries, irrespective of political ideologies or social systems, and their ability to maintain solidarity in spite of divergences of interest also reflected the wider coalition of Third World countries held together by common demands for a redistribution of wealth in their favor.

While historically accurate, this picture of the triumph of the poor countries over the rich may also be misleading. In actual fact major beneficiaries of the 200-mile exclusive economic zone will include several large developed countries, notably the United States, Canada, Australia, and the Soviet Union.[8] The United States, for example, will add 3 million square miles of territory, the largest acquisition in its history, and Canada will have its area expanded by more than 2.5 million square miles of sea and shelf territory.

A second irony is that only a small number of the developing countries, those with long coastlines and abundant off-coast natural resources, will benefit from the exclusive zones. A large number of the poorer countries will gain very little, since many are landlocked or shelf-locked and others have short coastlines or comparatively few resources off their coast. To these geographically disadvantaged countries, the large exclusive economic zones represent a betrayal of the idea of the *res communis* and common heritage.[9] However, their claims to an equitable share have not been unheeded, especially when it appeared that their voting strength could prevent adoption of a multinational treaty which requires a two-thirds majority. This has enhanced their collective bargaining power somewhat, leading to an explicit recognition of a right to participate in the exploration of the living resources in the economic zones of coastal states in the same region. There remains some doubt whether this "right" will be effectively implemented by coastal states, except where regional ties are strong or the geographically disadvantaged states have strong individual bargaining positions in respect to other issues.

Recognition of these various political and economic factors as determinants of multinational lawmaking does not mean that equitable considerations are immaterial or unimportant. I should like to underline this basic point once again. The fact that government actions are largely motivated by their conceptions of self-interest or material constraints does not alter the equity or inequity of the results in the minds of those affected by them. Their assessment of the fairness and justice of the arrangements is in itself a political fact of some importance since it will have a direct bearing on the tensions and conflicts that are likely to arise. Governments are mindful of this, and their debates on the economic zone reflect their views on equity as well as their self-interest. We can see how far governments are prepared to go by summarizing the principal propositions relevant to the exclusive economic zones which have received substantial support. These propositions indicate the extent to which conceptions of entitlement are linked to considerations of equity and material interests:

(1), the contiguity of land and marine environment creates situations of special dependence for coastal states on adjacent marine resources, and such dependence, especially when associated with basic needs for food supply, warrants their control over the resources;

(2), the exploitation of marine resources by distant countries is more likely to result in excessive depletion, waste, and pollution than would such exploitation by adjacent coastal countries with continuing dependence on those areas' marine resources;

(3), while the foregoing considerations favor coastal state resource jurisdiction, they need not entail any significant impairment of long-established freedoms of navigation and communication, and it remains in the common interest to assure such freedoms in the economic zones;

(4), the global needs for food supply require effective international standards and accountability for the conservation and maintenance of maximum sustainable yields of fish stocks;

(5), where coastal states do not have the capability to harvest the entire allowable catch, other states should be given access to the surplus of the catch;

(6), states which are landlocked or which, for other reasons, can have no exclusive economic zones should have rights to participate, on an equitable basis, in the exploitation of living resources in their regions;

(7), states which have for long periods habitually engaged in the exploitation of living resources within the newly established economic zones of others should be accorded preferred access to those areas if the resources are not being utilized to capacity;

(8), the delimitation of exclusive economic zones between opposite or adjacent states should be made on the basis of agreements that take into account equitable principles relevant to resources and special geographical conditions, as well as the normal equidistant rule;

(9), it would serve the interests of both equity and efficiency in some situations to provide for the sharing of benefits (normally in the form of revenues) in lieu of unrestricted access to fish stocks which are found in more than one exclusive zone or outside of any such zones;

(10), coastal states should make contributions to needy developing countries of a share of the revenues derived from exploitation of the oil and gas resources of the continental shelf in the area beyond 200 miles to the edge of the continental margin;

(11), the common global interest in safeguarding the oceans against ecological deterioration requires effective international standards and the accountability of the coastal states and others using the exclusive economic zones or exercising control over them.

It is clear from these propositions that the 200-mile zones, although designated as "exclusive," will not in fact involve full sovereignty or unlimited control of the coastal states. The coastal states will, however, have a wide range of authority. Their rights of management, use, and protection over resources are so extensive as to raise grave doubts whether they will be effectively limited by the international obligations imposed on them by the treaty.* Those doubts are a principal reason why many countries have sought mandatory provisions for third-party settlement of disputes. The United States, for example, has maintained that it could not accept the regime of the 200-mile economic zones

* Similar doubts will arise if the economic zones should be established through customary law, a probable development in the event a binding treaty is not achieved.

without the protection of a compulsory system of arbitral and judicial settlement. (I shall discuss this aspect below.) Some critics of the new system have suggested that the only effective way of assuring an equitable use of the ocean space in the economic zones (an area comprising more than one-third of the traditional area of the high seas) would be to place the entire area of ocean space beyond the 12-mile territorial sea under the managerial authority of an international body, with the benefits shared by all on the basis of contribution and need. As an alternative, it has been proposed that the system of free access and nonappropriability remain essentially in effect but be supplemented by international taxation or revenue-sharing arrangements for the benefit of the more needy countries.

It seems almost pointless, however, to dwell on these idealistic alternatives in the light of actual historical circumstances. The very fact that the area of the economic zones includes the most valuable resources of the sea—virtually all of the oil and gas and the greater part of harvestable fisheries—is an important reason why an international solution has found little favor in the coastal countries who stood to benefit from national control. As perceived by most coastal states the actual issue was how to eliminate or restrain a greedy "invader" who entered their adjacent waters to fish or obtain oil. (This is how New England fishermen saw the Soviet "invasion" of their waters.) The "invader" on the other hand saw its position as based on a historic or legal right to free access and as an equitable right to meet the needs of its people for food or energy. It is understandable that neither side was receptive to an international arrangement under which benefits would be shared with other states and under which authority would be exercised by a majority of other states and an unknown international agency. The victory of the coastal states was almost assured by their numerical preponderance over the "distant-water" fishing states combined with the fact that some of the latter (such as the United States and the USSR) have long coastlines and valuable fishery and nonliving resources in their adjacent waters. Moreover, the assurance to the shipping and naval interests of these and other maritime powers that passage for vessels in the economic zones and through straits would be unimpeded was still another significant factor in the acceptance of the scheme of exclusive economic zones. We should not expect this decision to be reversed for a very long time, if at all.

On the other hand, we can expect the new system to be subject to many strains and pressures. These will occur partly because conflicts and disputes will surely arise over different interpretations of the rights and obligations of the states concerned. The language of the treaty is replete with broad and vague standards relating to such diverse matters as participation of landlocked and geographically disadvantaged states in fishing in the zones, the demarcation of the boundaries of the zones ("in accordance with equitable principles"), or the rights of the coastal states to regulate shipping in the interest of preventing pollution. There can be little doubt that these issues and others will give rise to numerous differences over the application of general formulas to particular cases.

We can also be quite sure that the authority of the coastal states in the economic zones will be substantially affected by the necessities of international regulation. This will certainly be true of fisheries. One reason, of course, is that fish have little respect for man-made boundaries; another is that there is considerable biological interdependence between different species and different stocks of fish. Economic zone fisheries cannot be compartmentalized entirely and regional or global cooperation and regulation will be necessary. In the section on managerial regimes

I shall go into some of the problems that this raises.

We might also note that technological changes will affect the economic zones in ways that will require new rules and arrangements for international supervision. Energy is likely to be obtainable in the oceans through techniques that are still experimental but promise to be economic on a large scale eventually. For example, devices have been developed to produce energy through the great difference in temperature between surface and deep water. Also the biological production of energy through conversion of fast-growing marine plants into methane gas has practical possibilities. The well-known fact that tides, currents, and waves generate energy has stimulated numerous technological efforts. Of a somewhat different character would be the use of the oceans for the location of nuclear power plants. These diverse activities are likely to introduce impediments to other uses of the economic zones, such as navigation and fishing, and to affect the rights of the users or of the international community as a whole. While one cannot foresee the precise regulatory problems that will arise, it seems quite certain that international rules will be required.

One almost obvious conclusion to draw from these comments relating to the economic zones is that international machinery will be required to cope with the various problems likely to arise. Institutional means for settling disputes relating to the economic zones have received general support although the modalities have been the subject of much controversy. There have been advocates of a specialized Law of the Sea Tribunal, others who supported compulsory jurisdiction of the International Court of Justice, and still others who favored ad hoc arbitration. Since many important states, especially maritime powers, have demanded compulsory dispute settlement provisions as an essential condition of their acceptance of the exclusive economic zones, it is probable that arbitral or judicial settlement will be "required" under the new treaty.* It also seems quite certain that conciliation procedures will be recommended and perhaps required before more formal arbitration or judicial procedure may be utilized. The use of expert technical panels would also be advantageous in dealing with issues such as demarcation or the question of "optimal utilization" of fisheries in the economic zone. On the whole, informal procedures will probably be more widely used than judicial settlement for disputes over standards of equitable treatment. The role of the International Court of Justice will be less important in the early period than that of arbitral tribunals established by states on an ad hoc basis. As the body of law develops and more specificity is achieved in the regulatory norms, the advantages of recourse to a permanent judicial tribunal will become more apparent and the International Court may well assume a significant role.

There is also a need to establish institutional machinery to deal with problems through nonadversary means of settlement and through consideration of proposals for new or revised international rules. An intergovernmental organ, composed of all parties to the treaty, would be a desirable means for providing a systematic review of problems and proposing new arrangements. It could consider possible revision of the treaty at appropriate periodic intervals. Its work would be greatly aided by a permanent international secretariat which would furnish systematic information on practices and technical developments, carry out studies on problems arising under the treaty, and provide technical and advisory services of a nonpolitical character to governments, especially in the developing countries.

Though these international bodies would have no direct authority over activities in the economic zones, they

* The compulsory effect of dispute settlement clauses will probably be significantly reduced by allowing states to carve out exceptions through reservations.

could help to strengthen adherence to the equitable principles in the treaty and provide for adjustments to meet new conditions in coming years. It is not unlikely that they would grow in practical significance as they demonstrated their value in resolving conflicts and in facilitating cooperative arrangements for the beneficial uses of the economic zones.

Managerial Regimes
for Ocean Resources

Complicated as the issues are in regard to the exclusive economic zones, the problems of equitable sharing become even more complex when they relate to resources which do not entirely fall within those zones. These resources fall mainly into two categories: the valuable manganese nodules (containing nickel, copper, cobalt, and manganese) found in the deep seabed, and the migratory fish which move outside or across the exclusive zones. Each of these categories raises distinctive problems, but both are widely considered to require regulatory regimes of a managerial character. Once regarded as an essential principle of *res communis*, free and untrammeled access is now seen as superseded by the need for regulation to assure efficient and productive use and fair distribution of the benefits. This, it seems safe to say, expresses the position of most governments, and it holds true both for seabed mining and "nonexclusive" fisheries. However, differences arise once we go beyond this general proposition into the means of implementation and the nature of the regulatory regimes. These differences are varied, and they take many forms, but the main lines form, as might be expected, in the now characteristic division between the well-to-do industrialized states, on the one side, and the developing, technologically inferior states on the other. In the argument, industrialized countries stress greater productivity—the larger pie for all to share, though the shares may be unequal. The developing countries, on the other hand, emphasize equitable sharing related to their needs and international control through majority decisions. Underlying this general difference are conflicting attitudes as to the proper role of competition and market factors, the need for incentives for technological and capital investments, entry requirements, aims not related to efficient use (e.g., maintaining prices at high levels or providing employment opportunities), procedures for international decisions, and many more. The issues raised are not easy to resolve. For one thing, they involve conjecture about future developments in an uncertain economic and technical environment. It is not clearly known how individual countries will gain or lose from the anticipated developments or how much of a "social surplus" will be available for community use. Yet despite the uncertainties and differences of view, the pressures for international management in regard to both the seabed and global fisheries have considerable impact, and it seems likely that such regimes of one kind or another will be created. While definite predictions are hazardous at this point, the principal tendencies and specific proposals can be usefully examined from the standpoint of their relation to the objectives of equitable sharing and productive use of the common resources. I shall begin with seabed mining and after that consider fisheries arrangements.

Although complicated proposals have been made for a managerial regime for seabed mining, the issues can be most clearly perceived by contrasting the two competing approaches advanced at the inception of the prolonged multinational negotiations.[11] The first approach, supported

by the technologically advanced countries, proposed exploitation by various operating enterprises—public, private,
joint ventures, etc.—under a limited regime of international
licensing directed primarily toward maximum utilization of
seabed minerals within the technological and economic possibilities. The basic economic objective of this system would
be to achieve a competitive situation among producers, a
high level of output, and lower prices.[12] This result, it is
argued, would maximize benefits for all users of such minerals and for world economic development; in that practical
way, such a system would serve the goal of equitable sharing. In addition, the proponents of the approach agreed
that some share of the revenues should be made available,
through royalty payments, to a fund for the neediest countries. As a further concession to equity, it has also been
agreed that this fund may be used to compensate those
land-based producers of minerals who would lose in export
earnings as a result of the increased supply of ocean minerals. It is contended that these special revenue-sharing
provisions, together with the increased supply and lower
prices for all, would constitute a realistic and practical way
of realizing the benefits of the common heritage for all
states.

The competing approach, supported by the developing
countries and therefore by the large majority of states,
called for an international operating enterprise, under the
management of a Seabed Authority composed of all states,
to carry out all exploration and exploitation of mineral resources and also certain related activities, including the processing, transportation, and marketing of the products.[13]
To conduct its activities, the proposed authority and its operational enterprise would utilize service contracts with
technically qualified individuals and firms. Revenues would
be shared under a formula that would accord preferences

to the developing countries generally, to specially disadvantaged countries, and to those countries which would lose in earnings as a result of increased supply. One element in this conception would be the regulation of production, that is, the imposition of limits on output in order to maintain the prices and income of the developing countries engaged in land-based mining. It was proposed, and hoped, that the large financial and technological requirements for the proposed enterprise would be met mainly by the well-to-do developed countries in accordance with the general international policy of assisting the developing nations and furthering global development.

The proponents of this scheme for an international monopoly for seabed mining contend that under the alternative scheme of licensing, the operating enterprises would be mainly large transnational companies or national enterprises with sufficient power to escape effective regulation. These companies, it is charged, would tend to fix prices, allocate markets, and engage generally in oligopolistic restrictive practices directed toward increasing their own profits and power without regard to the needs or entitlements of the developing countries. In the words of an African delegate, "the dream of the common heritage of mankind will have been transformed into a reality of the common heritage of the multinational companies. It is to avoid this particular danger that the developing countries have insisted that the authority to be established should insure direct and effective control of all the activities in the area." [14]

A critical question that emerged from these two contending positions was whether or not the industrialized countries and the technologically qualified large enterprises would participate in the international Seabed Authority and its operational monopoly as proposed by the developing countries. If they would not, it appeared highly questionable whether the operating entity could succeed. The developing countries would then end up with a beached leviathan unable to function. This would be a long way from realizing the benefits of the common heritage. Even the land-based mining countries, which were less than enthusiastic about competition for seabed operations, would not benefit from this result because the industrialized countries would proceed independently to develop and produce the seabed minerals under tacit or express arrangements among themselves.*

In the light of these facts of power and technology, a compromise solution has emerged which seems likely to be adopted in the new treaty. That solution involves the elimination of the highly monopolistic character of the Seabed Authority by allowing national enterprises (including private companies) to carry out mining operations under terms and conditions specified in the treaty. Parallel systems would be established: some operations would be directly carried out by the authority through its own enterprise; and other operations by enterprises (including private firms) accorded security of tenure for a stated period subject to meeting standards of performance and other appropriate requirements. An interesting feature proposed for the parallel system of exploitation would require each contracting firm seeking authorization for mining operations to submit proposals for two mining sites of approximately equal size and value.[15] The authority would select one of these sites to be exploited by the authority directly (that is, by its operating enterprise) or made available to a developing country. The other site would then be licensed to the firm which had submitted the pair of sites. Through this arrangement, the authority would receive the benefit of the preferred site

* A legal premise for such action is that the seabed beyond national jurisdiction is not *res communis* but *res nullius* open to appropriation, irrespective of General Assembly declarations to the contrary.

based on the know-how of the individual firm in return for allowing the firm to operate on the other site selected by it. This is a classic equitable solution to a situation in which competing parties are unequal in knowledge and capability.

The basic condition of inequality among nations is at the heart of the problem of reaching an acceptable general decision-making system for the authority as a whole. The central issue concerns the power of the majority of states to determine policies, rules, and specific actions which may adversely affect the minority of countries, particularly those most directly involved as producers and sources of finance. Obviously, these countries would not enter into the basic treaty without safeguards which would not be alterable at the discretion of a majority. Since their participation is vital, concessions have to be made to them involving limits on majority rule. Three elements of an acceptable compromise have emerged in the negotiations.

First, the treaty itself would define the competence of the authority and its organs and the rights of the participating states and of the contracting firms in relation to the authority. These definitions would help to circumscribe the power of the authority to interfere with uses of the oceans outside of seabed mining, especially rights of passage and fishing. Another aim would be to prevent discrimination in granting licenses or contracts to enterprises seeking to carry out seabed mining. Still another important objective would be to place limitations on the authority's right to change the conditions of tenure and production. Such limitations would be necessary to attract firms required to make large investments of capital and technology in novel seabed operations. Clearly a strong case can be made on practical and equitable grounds for providing legal security by way of treaty safeguards. On the other hand, detailed treaty requirements should not rigidly prevent alterations required by changing technology and new needs. A procedure for adjustments in the seabed regime will be needed in due course and room must be left for interpretation by the organs of the authority. How to reconcile the need for adjustments with reasonable security for those who have to invest funds and know-how is a problem that cannot be solved through treaty provisions alone. It will require an acceptable system for checks and balances in the organs of the authority.

This involves the perennially difficult issue of the relationship of the plenary organ composed of all members to a smaller organ which functions as an executive body. A bicameral arrangement of this kind comprising an assembly and a council has been accepted for the Seabed Authority. The council would reflect in its composition of thirty-six members the special interests of certain states, especially those with advanced technology and those who have important interests as consumers or as land-based mining producers. While the precise formula still requires negotiation, the outlines of a solution on these lines are reasonably clear. The council would function as an executive organ with authority to lay down rules for operations and to supervise contracts and other operational activities. It is also anticipated that the council would have two important subsidiary organs—an economic planning commission and a technical commission—which would be composed of experts rather than governments. We can expect that the council, reflecting in its membership an appropriate mixture of countries with special interests as well as those geographically representative, will become the main center of decision making for the authority. However, since the council would have to conform to the general policies of the assembly and to its budgetary decisions, there will be elements of tension between the two principal organs which will reflect the actual conflicts of interest between the major groups of countries. Underlying these constitutional relations is the realistic requirement that the arrangement assure adequate opportunity for collective bargaining among the various interest groups and set limits to one-sided and arbitrary action. The provisions of the proposed treaty dealing with the organs of the Seabed Authority indicate that this requirement is well understood.

The third element in the compromise is provision for judicial review.[16] As envisaged, a permanent tribunal, composed of independent judges (elected in their personal capacity), would have jurisdiction over disputes relating to the interpretation and application of the treaty. Any state party to the treaty which questions the legality of measures taken by an organ of the authority would be entitled to bring the matter before the tribunal for a binding decision. The tribunal would also have competence to adjudicate disputes between the authority and states or firms with which the authority has entered into contracts and operating arrangements. Any such firm or any state concerned may bring the case to the tribunal even without agreement of the other party. Judgments of the tribunal would be final and binding. Advisory opinions would also be possible on request of an organ of the authority in respect to any legal question connected with the subject matter of the treaty. These provisions for judicial review of the authority's acts and for compulsory adjudicative procedures in regard to contracts are significant elements in the bargain being struck between the developing country majority and the minority of countries with technological and financial power. They provide some assurance that the operations of the authority will not be wholly determined by political coalitions or transitory pressures. On the other hand, they may give rise to concern that a tribunal composed of a few individuals could thwart the general will of states or determine issues of policy on narrow legalistic grounds. While that concern cannot be dismissed out of hand, the danger of judicial obstructionism is not likely to be serious. The judges will be selected by the political organs of the authority from among persons nominated by the states. Their term of office will be limited, probably to five years. It is hard to believe that they will be insensitive to the political will expressed in the organs or that they would override legislative or executive measures which have reasonable bases in law and fact. It is perhaps more questionable whether they will show the necessary judicial independence when the issues of treaty interpretation or of contractual terms are delicate and not easily resolved on technical legal grounds. Even with this doubt the availability of judicial procedures may provide some measure of security to states and firms which have an interest in the observance of the treaty provisions and in preventing arbitrary or capricious decisions by the authority.

The task of establishing a managerial regime for global fishing presents problems rather different from those raised in regard to seabed mining. For one thing, there is little support for a global management authority for all fisheries outside of national jurisdiction. It is, however, true that among governments and the fishing industry there is increased recognition that the traditional system of open access needs to be substantially replaced by a managerial system. Virtually no one would deny that free access and unlimited competition have resulted in considerable overfishing and economic waste. As was observed earlier, more and more capital and manpower are pursuing fewer fish. In some cases, the depletion of stocks has gone below the biological sustainable yield. It is widely agreed that regulations are required to govern the fishing effort (as, for example, by gear restrictions, size limitations, seasonal restrictions, closed areas) and to provide for flexible authority to impose controls and allocate rights to fish.[17] However, unlike the case of seabed mining, it is not feasible to have a centralized management authority in view of the diverse biological and economic settings for fisheries.

A more acceptable pattern of management would allow for a variety of international arrangements to cover fishing which involved stocks outside of coastal state exclusive zones and those which—as in many cases—move through the zones of two or more states. Typically, two or more neighboring states would establish management commissions for the appropriate geographical areas or for a particular stock or species within those areas. Arrangements of a wider regional character (such as North Atlantic) or of a global character would be desirable for a specific migratory stock or species. The special situation of anadromous and catadromous species would call for management arrangements between the coastal states principally concerned and the countries which fish for those species on the high seas. In short, the jurisdictional bases for the various management regimes should be determined by the particular features of the fishing industry involved. It would be desirable to avoid jurisdictional difficulties between various management authorities with overlapping areas through consultative and dispute-settlement provisions.

Even if jurisdiction and authority are clear, the issues of equitable sharing likely to arise in such international fisheries regimes will not be easy to resolve. One complex problem concerns the allocation rights to fishermen of states that are not members of the managerial entity. For example, should the distant-water fleets of large fishing states have rights based on their prior use or their needs? What of new entrants? Two approaches have been suggested: one would place the management authority under

an obligation to permit external fishing vessels under specified criteria (most importantly, when there is underutiliza-
tion of the resources by the fishermen of the member
states); the alternative approach would give the management authority exclusive rights but with the power to permit external entry on conditions it sets. Under the second
approach, the management authority would be expected to
negotiate with the external fishermen in order to utilize the
fish stocks fully and maximize benefits. It has been pointed
out that under the first "mandatory" system, the negotiations for entry would take place through interpretation of
the criteria.[18] On the second "permissive" system, the bargaining and negotiating would take place not by the interpretation of rules but by dealing more directly with the proposed external effort and its contribution. This might seem
inequitable in the sense that outsiders would have no determinate rights even when the fisheries were on the high seas
entirely outside of coastal state limits. A possible solution
for this situation would be to provide for revenue sharing in
the "social surplus" for the benefit of all states, particularly
the developing countries. Similar revenue sharing might
also be applied to countries sharing coastal fisheries which
do not participate in the fishing effort. Such revenue-sharing funds made up of royalty or tax payments (over and
above the costs of management) would meet the demand
for equitable sharing by the states entitled to the common
resource (whether this is on a global, regional, or
subregional basis).

The question of the rights to fish of prior users, especially those with historic rights or well-founded special
needs, will have to be faced wherever new management
regimes are set up or where new jurisdictional rights are
granted to existing bodies. An abrupt exclusion of "outside"
fishing fleets which have long harvested the fishing stocks

concerned would be unjust and almost certain to create hardship. Even a gradual reduction might be a hardship where the external fishing state is highly dependent on the resource for its food supply (as may be true for Japan in some areas). Obviously, this consideration should not prevail when there is a serious danger of early depletion and a drastic reduction in catch is considered necessary. However, in most cases the special circumstances of need and prior investment should be given consideration so as to reduce economic dislocation. The imposition of increased fees and royalties on the external fleet may be a practicable way of compensating the states within the managerial regime without causing undue hardship for the dependent external fishing industry. In general, a strong case can be made for separating the right to benefits from the rights of access. There is, in fact, one example of an international arrangement based on that separation: the agreement concerning the fur seals in the North Pacific. Under that agreement, the seals are harvested only by the countries on whose islands they breed, i.e., the USSR and the United States. The states that previously caught the seals on the high seas agreed to abstain from doing so, and in return they receive a share of the skins. Through this treaty arrangement, the wasteful practice of hunting the seals on the high seas has been eliminated, and the total catch has been increased. These advantages have been realized because the main objective is the economic benefit to be shared and maximized rather than the historic right of freedom to fish.

This brings us to the more basic question of the primary criterion of management. Historically, under international agreements this has been the maximum sustainable yield from a given stock of fish. That criterion has been criticized as unsatisfactory because it does not take account of costs and often leads to the prohibition of more efficient fishing gear. Moreover, a maximum yield is not a sufficient criterion where two or more stocks of fish are competing for the same food so that the yield of only one can be maximized. For these and other reasons, resource economists have maintained that the main criterion for a fisheries managerial regime should be the maximization of the net economic return (or the "rent of the sea").[19] This aim must, of course, include the maintenance of the fish stock as a resource but by emphasizing the economic return, not the physical maximum, it takes account of the need to limit costs and to avoid inefficient devices and economic waste in regulating the catch. The economic criterion also provides a basis for comparison among the different species of fish which may be in competition. Moreover, by measuring the benefits (or the wealth) of fish stocks in terms of economic revenues rather than rights to fish or tonnage, it becomes far easier to provide for sharing on the basis of equitable considerations and the principle of the common heritage. Revenue sharing can be facilitated through the use of monetary payments to build a common fund for distribution. The use of the economic criterion does not remove the necessity for allocating fishing opportunities when free access is no longer permitted, nor does it avoid the decision on the division of the economic rents collected. These tasks still have to be faced, but they are facilitated because economic revenue is a much more flexible standard than physical maxima.

Although the foregoing considerations are persuasive, it should be recognized that the objectives of governments in respect to fisheries cannot be reduced to the sole aim of maximizing economic rent.[20] Values of a noneconomic character are often important (for example, a local community or indigenous people may be dependent on fishing rights), and these values vary for individual countries and regions. The fisheries' managerial regimes should recognize diverse goals, and they should seek to optimize them to the extent possible. However, in view of the historical conditions which have promoted waste and inefficiency in fishing and have impeded a fair sharing of benefits, it is generally desirable to seek to maximize economic benefits and assure their wide distribution among the states entitled to them.

Although I have discussed these matters in general terms, it is well to remember that fisheries problems will be largely dealt with by neighboring countries or by other small groups of states. In consequence, the broad standards prescribed by treaty will usually be varied to meet local circumstances. There are advantages to such pluralism since it allows for flexible adaptation to particular conditions and also for experimentation. On the other hand, there may be disadvantages for weaker countries (for example, land-locked states) unable to bring about compliance with the equitable principles and standards adopted in the general treaty. Dispute-settlement procedures, such as those discussed earlier, may prove to be helpful to redress injustices in some cases. It may also be desirable to devise arrangements through which regional or "special interest" organs for fisheries or other ocean resources could be scrutinized by the global bodies which are concerned with the common interest and with the implementation of general standards. This would not only afford recourse to weaker members of the regional or specialized bodies and to nonmembers who might be prejudiced by those bodies but it should also help to develop universal norms of fair practice among states of unequal wealth and power.

Equitable Apportionment of Freshwater Resources

The dilemmas of equitable sharing have long been apparent in regard to the use of rivers and lakes common to two or more states. Criteria of prior use, of historic rights, and of relative needs have been advanced as equitable standards and have been invoked in numerous controversies between neighboring states. This has been reflected not as much in judicial or arbitral decisions as in the literature of international law and in the many inter-state bodies, beginning with the Danube River Commission, which was the first of modern international organizations.[21] Until recent years questions of navigation were the main issues, but now the more important and controversial problems relate to the use of water for agriculture and industry. The vast expansion of the demand for water, the reduction of supply due to natural and man-made causes, and the increased impairment of the quality of water have combined to place freshwater requirements in the forefront of international resource problems; indeed, as a group of United Nations experts have suggested, water may well have become "the major long-term natural resources problem of mankind." [22]

Moreover, as a consequence of increased scientific knowledge about hydrological systems and the multiple uses of water for expanding agricultural and industrial needs, new content and significance have been given to the general principle of equitable use and appropriation which has long been accepted as the basic standard for international water sharing. The claims for equitable treatment by competing users have intensified with increased demand and with actual or potential scarcity. As in the case of the oceans, the interplay of economic, technological, and normative factors is producing new legal concepts and arrangements that combine ideas of distributive justice and of practical resource management.

Of central importance in this development is the wider conception of international water resources expressed in the notion of the international drainage basin and, in some cases, by the still broader concept of the hydrosystem. The drainage basin is significant because it includes the underground waters physically connected with the surface waters. Such underground waters are far more extensive than the international rivers and lakes. In fact, it has been estimated that ground water represents 95 percent of the manageable fresh water supply of the globe, and there are about 170 international drainage basins.[23] The use of the drainage basin as the territorial unit for sharing does more than delimit a geographical area; it brings within the scope of shareability the whole system of surface and underground hydrological linkages which affect the availability and the quantity of water. In the words of a United Nations report, "all of man's and nature's works within the basin affect alterations, directly or indirectly, in the water's quantity, quality or rate and timing of flow. These changes in the behavior of the hydrosystem may be felt in distant points in the basin." [24] For this reason, it is neither fair nor sensible to apply international standards of equitable use only to a part of the interconnected waters of an international drainage basin.

It is also beginning to be realized that the equitable use of international water resources may have to include atmospheric water. This has been apparent as drought and desertification have increased in various parts of the globe due to changes in precipitation arising from various causes. From a scientific standpoint, the fact of "hydro-interdependence" extends to the entire water cycle or system whether on the surface, underground, or in the atmosphere and, accordingly, an international water resource system "includes all the territory within which water occurs or flows as part of a physically interconnected international system." [25] This broader concept will become practically relevant for international cooperation and regulation to the extent to which the atmospheric water segment can be manipulated or modified. This is not an unlikely technological development for the future, and it does not seem too soon to consider the political problems and the uses of equitable distribution that would be involved in such atmospheric modifications. But, apart from that aspect, the international drainage basin can serve as an appropriate basis of international regulation.

The use of the drainage basin (or hydrosystem) as a key concept also has implications for the allocation of waters that go beyond its broader physical scope. It serves to underline the idea of unity and of integrated development. At least implicitly it indicates that allocation among various uses should give a high degree of priority to maximizing the benefits of the basin as a whole. While this principle of maximization cannot function as a categorical rule without further specification, it points to the importance of avoiding relatively wasteful uses and to the desirability of a unified and comprehensive scheme for use by all the parties. When supply is inadequate criteria of distribution will still be required, and for this purpose equitable standards based on respective needs and legitimate expectations will normally be applied. A useful checklist of relevant factors is contained in the Helsinki rules adopted by the International Law Association.[26] They include, inter alia, consideration of the past and present utilization of waters of the basin; the economic and social needs of each basin state; the extent of the dependence of the population of each basin state upon the waters of the basin; the comparative costs of alternative means of satisfying the economic and social needs of each basin state; the availability of other resources; the avoidance of unnecessary waste in the utilization of the waters of the basin; the practicability of compensation to one or more of the co-basin states as a means of adjusting conflict among uses; the degree to which the needs of a basin state may be satisfied without causing substantial injury to a co-basin state. Under these rules the weight of each factor is to be determined in each case; no use is entitled to any inherent preference over other uses. On the other hand, some international agreements—e.g., the U.S.-Canadian Boundary Waters Treaty of 1909—establish an order of preference among uses. In several other arrangements, preference is given to existing uses. But, on the whole, the approach of the Helsinki rules, involving a balancing of equities, is reasonable and seems likely to prevail both in customary law situations and in the interpretation of general treaty provisions on equitable use.[27]

It will be necessary, however, to add some new factors to the list of those to be taken into account for purposes of equitable apportionment. In most situations, consideration should be given to the environmental consequences and the wider interest of the global or regional community in preventing unreasonable pollution and in preserving the integrity of ecosystems. The importance of the quality of the water as well as the quantity and rate of flow has become increasingly evident in all parts of the world. A good illustration is provided by the prolonged dispute between the United States and Mexico which arose because of the increased salinity of the Colorado River flow into Mexico, a dispute finally settled by an agreement in 1973.[28] It is surprising that the basic treaty of 1944 on the Colorado River, which took years to negotiate, dealt only with the quantum of water and was entirely silent as to its quality (although the treaty refers to agriculture as one of the purposes for which the water would be used by Mexico). By 1961 it had become apparent that new drainage and irrigation projects had caused a drastic increase in the salt content of the water reaching Mexico, with disastrous consequences to farming in the Mexicali valley. The United States, which first rested its case on the literal terms of the treaty (but avoided proposed arbitration), eventually recognized, after much political pressure by Mexico, the reasonableness of the Mexican position that Mexico was entitled to usable water for agriculture. Under the 1973 agreement, there is to be a desalination plant, and other steps will be taken to reduce salinity and to deliver water of a quality not inferior to that previously received. The case points up the not uncommon effect of irrigation in degrading the quality of water, especially in arid areas (evidenced also by the disasters of increased salinity in the much-lauded Indus River project). Joint planning and a common approach would undoubtedly help to avoid crises, but they would have little effect unless the upper riparian state complied with its obligation to exercise restraints so as to meet the reasonable entitlements to usable water of the lower riparian state. This point merits emphasis because of a current tendency to assume that administrative procedures are in themselves sufficient to solve difficulties independently of substantive criteria.

It is reasonable, however, that procedural requirements should be regarded as essential to the equitable sharing of water resources. They have particular importance because of the breadth and flexibility of the formulae for equitable use and appropriation. In the absence of hard and precise rules for allocation, there is a relatively greater need for specifying requirements for advance notice, consultation, and decision procedures. Such requirements are, in fact, commonly found in agreements by neighboring states concerning common lakes and rivers.[29] Recent trends, particularly in the wake of heightened environmental concerns, suggest the eventual emergence of a general rule of international law for a "system of information and prior consultation" in regard to the utilization of the common resources of two or more states. However, the resistance to a general rule, especially to one of wide scope, should not be underestimated. At the 1972 Stockholm Conference on the Environment, a proposal recommending prior consultation was defeated after a major debate (particularly between Brazil and Argentina concerning a Brazilian hydroelectric project in the upper tributaries of the Plata River basin). Subsequently, a softer proposal calling for cooperation on the basis of prior information and consultation in case of common resources was adopted by the General Assembly.[30] If this should evolve into a definite legal requirement, it would have to be given further specification in regard to the timing and contents of the advanced notification, the data and investigations to be made before the project can be undertaken, the scope of consultation (for example, should local authorities be involved?), and so on.[31] These are all matters which depend on the particular circumstances and do not lend themselves to rules of general import. Problems of adequacy of data may be especially difficult in large-scale hydrological projects. It is not difficult to point to several projects (e.g., Indus River or Aswan) where considerable unforeseen damage occurred because of inadequate information. On the other hand, measures to avoid procrastinating tactics are necessary, though not easy to devise (particularly in the absence of third-party determinations) when numerous factors are involved and the true limits must depend on the particular circumstances. Nor would it be a simple matter to provide for adequate sanctions if a party goes ahead without complying with adequate notice and consultation requirements.

In most cases these difficulties can be alleviated, if not entirely overcome, not only through joint institutional arrangements for continuous cooperation on the technical level but also by the local entities directly affected by the proposed action. The more or less routine interchange of data, frequent contact among technicians, and joint studies and investigations are practical ways of acquiring timely information and minimizing international procrastination or hasty action. The establishment of joint technical commissions is the obvious way for neighboring states to accomplish such technical cooperation. But steps can also be taken without establishing commissions, as, for example, by designating officials of the national ministries and agencies responsible for water resource management to exchange information and carry out the joint inquiries and consultation similar to those done by the commissions.[32] In time, separate bodies may emerge for continuous joint planning and consultations.

The future development of mixed commissions for international drainage basins should obviously benefit from the considerable experience acquired in the past fifty years. There are approximately one hundred such joint commissions concerned with nonnavigational works for the use of international water resources (still others, mainly the older ones, are limited to navigation), and they go back as far as 1816 when a German-Netherlands body was set up in regard to the Rhine River works. More than half of these commissions are in Europe (fifty-five), about twenty in America, nine in Asia, and five in Africa.[33] The International Joint Commission established by the United States and Canada under the Boundary Waters Treaty of 1909 has been one of the most successful, reaching agreement in nearly all of the one hundred or so cases submitted to it.[34] The use by that commission of technical boards of experts acting in a professional capacity has helped to avoid, even in acrimonious controversies, serious disturbances of intergovernmental relations. It is also instructive that the International Joint Commission has had to go beyond the functions of data collection, exchange of information, assessment, and consultation when dealing with especially difficult situations such as apportionment of the benefits of the Columbia River development and the still more complex problems concerning pollution of the Great Lakes.[35] In these cases, it was necessary to have substantive criteria as a frame of reference for quasi-adjudicative and regulatory action. If such mixed commissions are to take measures for equitable sharing, rational use, and the prevention and settlement of disputes in respect of common water resources, they will generally require licensing authority (as many have) and rule-making powers. Provisions for the judicial review of licensing and for governmental veto of rules where the political or economic consequences are important would seem advisable in most cases. One must bear in mind that the issues in water sharing involve more than finding facts or exchanging data and views. They require giving up valuable, often vital, resources and resolving competing entitlements. The procedures and the substantive law of the mixed commissions must be adequate for those issues.

Although mixed commissions of the states concerned are most appropriate for the management of shared drainage basins, they should probably be supplemented by international arrangements of a wider geographical and functional scope. The Nordic Environmental Protection Convention of 1974 and the OECD provide examples that can be followed more generally in global international agencies concerned with environmental protection. In the OECD, the secretariat, or a member state can set in motion a "confrontation mechanism" when potentially harmful chemical compounds are to be introduced. Such a procedure could be used more generally to assess the environmental impact of proposed alterations affecting the supply or quality of waters of transnational concern. At the global level, The United Nations Environment Programme (UNEP) would provide a suitable context for this kind of consultative process to take place.[36] Because of the global concern of the UNEP, its competence would extend to all the ecological aspects of different human activities affecting the supply of water, not just the environmental impact of works and development activities in international drainage basins. For example, the growing concern over pollution in the oceans and the fact that much of this pollution is a result of river discharges highlight the deficiency of existing international concepts and agreements which aim at reconciling and protecting the equal rights of co-basin states or, at most, optimizing utilization for the benefit of the "basin community." Following the OECD model, the UNEP secretariat could initiate a "confrontation" and prepare impact studies with a view to assessing the potential risks to the global marine environment of waste disposal into rivers. Thereby, a new and needed relationship would be established between the utilization of a drainage basin on the one hand, and the protection of other resources and wider environmental interests on the other.

The experience derived from the collaborative mechanisms relating to rivers and drainage basins is likely to be used as a guideline for other resources shared by a limited number of states. Some first steps in this direction have been taken within the UNEP where proposals for a code of conduct for such common resources have been under consideration.[37] It has been suggested that a code of this kind should be devised from practice evidenced in bilateral and multilateral arrangements as well as from the writings of eminent jurists and other experts. A basic principle would uphold the responsibility of all states to ensure that the exercise of their right to exploit resources within their jurisdiction does not cause damage to the environment of other states or of areas beyond the limits of national jurisdiction. The code would spell out the rules for advance notice, exchange of information, and consultation. It would, for example, define the circumstances under which notice would be required, its timeliness, the kind of data to be furnished, the conditions of consultation, the avoidance of unreasonable delays, and similar matters. Also envisaged as elements of the proposed code are procedures for emergency action, for settlement of disputes, and for liability and compensation to foreign victims. It would be understood that the provisions of the code would apply generally in the absence of relevant bilateral or multilateral agreements.

The idea of a code underlines the value of general normative principles expressed as law, or even as proposed law, in providing a coherent and balanced framework for practical cooperation. Moreover, it is a reminder that legal concepts and procedures can be utilized to give specificity and clarity to the broad aims of equitable sharing and harmonious management of common resources. Whether a binding legal code is achieved or simply guidelines to influence state practice and special agreements, it seems clear that a body of international property law is emerging for the sharing of the varied resources common to two or more states in all parts of the world. On the present indications, it would not be too optimistic to regard this development as a major step toward the practical realization of the idea of equitable use and appropriation for resources of vital importance to a large part of mankind.

The Atmosphere
and the Global Environment

In contrast to the familiar conception of the high seas as *res communis,* the idea of the atmosphere and of weather and climate conditions as "international commons" may seem somewhat farfetched. For one thing, we are accustomed to the legal principle that the airspace over a country is part of its national territory and entirely under its authority. In addition, weather and climate are not generally perceived as physical resources capable of being used or exploited. Yet, with new technologies, greater scientific knowledge, and the wastes of industrial civilization, our conceptions are beginning to change. Modifications of the atmosphere by one country, whether deliberate or inadvertent, are increasingly seen as consequential to other countries and as requiring standards of international responsibility. International lawyers may point with some pride to their early recognition of the problem, particularly in the wake of the much-cited Trail Smelter arbitration award of 1941 which held that the emission of sulphur fumes into the atmosphere in Canada, which were proven injurious to persons in nearby areas of the United States, constituted an international wrong.[38] Although that ruling still stands in splendid isolation, international jurists have amply used it as the foundation stone of an expanded notion of international responsibility for damage caused through the airspace to persons outside of the originating state.[39] This has contributed, in some degree, to an international awareness of the shareability of the atmosphere, but it is only one element in a varied pattern of influences. The most important factors are those scientific and technological advances which have made us aware that the atmosphere, weather, and climate are usable resources subject to manipulation by human endeavors with consequences that extend far beyond national frontiers.

This is perhaps most evident in respect of measures deliberately undertaken to modify weather and climate. Best known are cloud seedings to increase rainfall (which may reduce needed precipitation in other areas) and the more dramatic attempts to mitigate the effects of hurricanes, typhoons, and cyclones. Though these efforts are beneficial, they may also adversely affect some countries as the path of the storm is changed and winds and accompanying rains diverted.[40] Of even more concern are proposed activities which may involve modifications in climate and weather on a vast scale. The most commonly discussed are schemes to reduce the Arctic ice cap by placing heat-absorbing material (such as soot) on the ice or generating clouds over the Arctic to trap heat.[41] While reduction of the Arctic ice cap could bring considerable benefit to some areas, it is feared that melting of large portions of the cap might have serious consequences and possibly cause disasters in many areas. Long-term changes in precipitation, in wind systems, and sea levels are seen as distinct possibilities. Finally, the potential use of weather modifications for hostile military purposes, already evidenced on a limited scale, is another source of concern.[42]

International anxiety has also been manifested in regard to the possible effects on the weather and climate of human activities not intentionally directed toward weather modification.[43] Projects which would alter important natural ecological systems such as the destruction of large forests, mountain ranges, and glaciers are feared as threats to existing weather and climate conditions in distant areas. Similarly, the diversion of large rivers or the creation of huge lakes, both within the realm of present capabilities, would probably involve major changes in the atmospheric conditions outside of the countries undertaking these projects. The most likely dangers of large-scale modifications—and the most difficult to prevent—are those which arise from the cumulative effects of industrialization, urbanization, and certain agricultural practices. Although the scientific literature is far from definitive on these effects, and conflicting appraisals are not unusual, there are reasons for apprehension over the increases in carbon dioxide and dust, the effects on the ozone, and the apparent changes in wind circulation resulting from the impact of recent economic developments. The increased incidence of drought and desertification in many areas and of floods in others has added urgency to this concern.

Taken together, these diverse elements have focused attention on the systemic physical interconnections of airspace, weather, and climate and on the necessity for international regulatory measures.[44] Inasmuch as gains and losses are involved, often on a considerable scale, proposed regulatory measures implicitly raise questions of equitable sharing. This becomes quite clear in cases of the diversion of storms which benefit some and risk injury to others or in proposed large-scale engineering projects such as changing river flows. The issues are not quite as sharp in regard to the cumulative effects of industrialization or other continuous activities which have unintended and still uncertain adverse effects. Yet even in such cases the issue of equity has been raised, both by claims of the less-developed countries that the industrialized world should compensate others for environmental damage and by arguments that future generations are being deprived of their heritage. The problems of dealing with this general and diffuse issue of equitable sharing are, of course, substantially different from the questions raised by specific projects. The two sets of questions will be discussed separately.

With respect to specific projects of weather modification, the aim of equitable treatment of those adversely affected can be served, in the first instance, by requiring certain procedures—in particular, advance notification and consultation.[45] This has indeed been proposed by UN bodies as a general principle involving resources common to two or more states.[46] In respect to weather modification, the air shed or air mass over neighboring states could appropriately be considered a common resource subject to the proposed requirement of notice and consultation. As weather technology is used more frequently and widely, procedures beyond consultation may also be required. It would be reasonable for regional groups of states to establish commissions to which the affected parties could appeal prior to a proposed action. Such commissions could be either joint bodies of the states concerned (like the river commissions) or panels of experts qualified to evaluate the proposed action. The latter would be more appropriate in view of the need to pass on technical matters that are still in an uncertain stage of knowledge. In general, the functions of such commissions would include evaluating effects, drafting proposals to mitigate damage (including, if necessary, proposals prohibiting a project), and fixing compensation. It would not be unreasonable to divide such tasks between technical bodies which would pass upon the possible dangers and seek technical solutions and mixed commissions of an adjudicative character which would assess liability and determine the damages to be paid. While these procedural measures appear to be the minimum necessary to assure protection and fair treatment, we should not expect them to be adopted as easily as were similar arrangements for common water resources. An important difference is that in the case of river drainage basins, the reciprocal element is clear; shareability is recognized, and the standard of equitable use and appropriation is generally accepted. In the case of atmospheric and weather projects, reciprocity is not as clear, since only technically advanced countries have the capability of meteorological intervention, and they may not feel threatened by interventions of other countries. But we can expect this to change as meteorological interventions become more frequent and effective with a greater impact on many countries. We can also assume that international concern expressed in the United Nations and in regional bodies will influence the active states to accept procedural arrangements, especially for situations involving limited areas and well-defined intentional actions affecting weather.

Procedural arrangements, even the most minimal, will entail some reference to criteria of equity in determining whether a project should proceed. A typical question would be whether a proposed action to prevent large-scale damage by a hurricane should be called off because it would reduce rainfall elsewhere in some uncertain degree.[47] Indeed, almost every case will involve some balancing of the benefits to one country against the possible damage or risks to another. It is most unlikely that hard and fast rules could be applied. For example, a rule analogous to the "prior use" principle applied to river projects would not be reasonable for these cases. On the other hand, a list of the relevant factors to be considered in such cases would be useful and might help to achieve a wider acceptance of consultative and commission arrangements. It does not seem unlikely that such arrangements will be adopted for the limited class of meteorological actions that are clearly likely to affect neighboring countries. They will form a part of the growing *droit du voisinage* responsive to environmental concerns.

This rather optimistic prognosis cannot so easily be made for the ecological interventions which take place on a large scale and which are not clearly circumscribed in their effects. Such interventions include, as indicated earlier, on the one hand, identifiable discrete projects such as building large lakes, eliminating forests, or rerouting large rivers. On the other hand, they include the cumulative results of industrial development, agricultural practices, and urban growth. In the case of the first group—the discrete projects—we can see certain obstacles to regulatory arrangements of the kind discussed for limited weather modification. One is that the projects are major internal development projects which are conceived to bring substantial long-range benefits to a great many people within a country. Such projects are regarded as falling within the sovereign rights of states to exploit their own resources freely. By and large, the adverse consequences that may occur elsewhere will not be definitively ascertainable and are likely to involve considerable scientific conjecture. Moreover, the very fact of these uncertainties and the risks of irreversible effects on large parts of the globe and into the future (as by changing rainfall) would generally require an outright prohibition. The issues thus presented are difficult to compromise. They cannot be solved by compensation or by technical changes; nor would the balancing of relative needs be an easily acceptable way of resolving the issues of entitlement and sovereign rights. At the same time, the enormity of the risks—especially the danger of large-scale drought and flooding—that would result from some of the ambitious projects proposed by scientists and engineers may generate an acute sense of international urgency and alarm. The existence of a United Nations "watchdog" agency, the United Nations Environmental Programme, which has a growing global information system, will add substance to such international anxieties when specific projects which threaten large-scale risks are made known.[48] One step which may be undertaken is the establishment of an authoritative body of scientists and other experts to evaluate the risks of proposed projects based on a requirement of prior notification. A precedent for this can be found in the field of outer space where an expert panel known as COSPAR, established by the International Council of Scientific Unions (ICSU), has the function of determining whether activities in outer space would be injurious. Under the Outer Space

Treaty, international consultation is required in respect to proposed experiments or other potentially harmful activities in space.[49] Although COSPAR does not have the authority to prohibit such activities, the scientific weight of its pronouncements would undoubtedly have considerable influence. However, we should recognize that the issues will be of more practical import in the case of large-scale developmental projects than in regard to outer space and consequently that compliance with the findings of an international scientific panel may be resisted by national authorities. But here, too, there is a counteracting factor— namely, that the global dangers of ecological damage will probably be more consequential to many countries and therefore international opinion may be more effectively mobilized to support the negative findings of scientists. In any case, there are good reasons for moving toward a procedure for international scientific evaluation and for international accountability in respect to the far-reaching projects that may affect weather and climate over large areas of the globe. The ultimate aim should be a general prohibition of such projects unless they are approved by an authoritative panel on the basis of well-substantiated findings.

What about the claim that in some cases such projects could be justified on the basis of the classic utilitarian formula of the greatest good of the greatest number? This could obviously lead to the harsh conclusion that relatively small groups of peoples could be subjected to threat of famine so that large and populous countries would improve the lot of their more numerous inhabitants. I would hope that this form of international utilitarianism, which threatens genocidal consequences, would be regarded as intolerable. The principle of nonintervention should be applied to exclude those major environmental modifications in one country which would cause deprivation on a serious scale elsewhere.

The only exception should be the necessity of saving human lives, where clearly demonstrated. It would not be reasonable to apply this basic principle by requiring the consent of all states that may be affected—in effect, granting a veto right—as long as it is possible to have an authoritative international body to pass upon the proposed action.

A far more difficult problem of international regulation is presented by our other category of atmospheric modification—namely, the cumulative impact of human activities threatening serious consequences to ecological patterns and especially rainfall and other climatic factors. Most of the dangers in this category result from industrialization, urbanization, and the expansion of agriculture. These activities obviously cannot be prohibited nor can they be curtailed without imposing great hardships, generally on the most disadvantaged groups.[50] Their long-run consequences are still not sufficiently clear as to qualify such activities as clear and present dangers. But it is almost certainly necessary to develop a more adequate international informational and monitorial process to discover specific dangers (e.g., threats to the ozone or overheating due to carbon dioxide) so that measures of mitigation can be applied.

Implicit in mitigation—though this is not often appreciated—is the appraisal of relative equities: who should make the sacrifices and on what criteria of fairness and justice? These are not simply questions of a technical character. The dilemmas of equitable sharing we discussed in Part I will arise in these cases. In many cases, it would be in keeping with the principles asserted by international bodies to seek solutions which would satisfy the basic human needs of the most deprived groups and impose sacrifices on those relatively well-off. This may involve the assumption of some ecological risks to prevent reductions in the standard of life of the severely disadvantaged groups. A less drastic measure of mitigation would be to reduce those conveniences and consumption habits in the developed countries which provide relatively minor benefits and present potential threats. An example of current interest is the widespread use of aerosol-spraying devices which are said to impair the protective qualities of the ozone.[51] If that apprehension is well-founded, it would be difficult to object to the prohibition of those devices. But this relatively easy case does not carry us very far toward an answer for the more pervasive and difficult problem of coping with the cumulative effects of industrialization. No formula or rule can be prescribed for the limits beyond which beneficial activities should be reduced because of the long-range cumulative effects at some future time. Even if present estimates suggest increased risks, they are not sufficient to impose substantial restraints that would justify the deprivations resulting from the large-scale curtailment of productive activity. What they do clearly call for are more extensive surveillance, research, and evaluation of the impact of such productive activity on the global environment. Along with that, they call for an increased awareness of the common interest in a habitable world and of the priority of that interest over local and short-range benefits. It falls largely to international governmental bodies and to scientific associations to give practical effect to these objectives.

Part III
Equity
in
Distribution

IN the present chapter, we turn to issues which are at the heart of the controversies over distribution of the world's product. They relate particularly to the pricing of raw materials, monopolistic and oligopolistic restraints, the transfer of technology and the relocation of industry, the regulation of multinational companies and foreign investors, and the responsibility to prevent famine and malnutrition. These are all issues characterized by clashes of interest between the industrialized and the developing countries and by grievances reflecting basic attitudes as to what is fair and just. At the same time, they are the subject matter for new forms of international cooperation designed to meet economic scarcities, dislocation, and political demands. As we have previously observed, such arrangements, whether highly structured or not, necessarily include criteria, rules, and procedures to guide or determine decisions, and these can be said to constitute "law" in a functional and realistic sense. Moreover, within the context of the particular arrangements as well as on a more general level, issues of equity are presented which call for normative judgments and give rise to the emergence of new criteria.

In the discussion that follows, I shall present these developments, not as the unfolding of abstract notions of equity, but as the products of conflict and bargaining, influenced by material conditions and the requirements of collective decision. But we should not forget that the international instrumentalities can—and surely will—be judged by their relation to the ideas of equity which shape the demands and expectations of the human beings affected by them.

Just Prices

A conspicuous feature of the current demands for a more equitable economic order is the idea of "just prices" or, more broadly, a just relationship of prices.[1] Although the conception of a just price goes back to medieval philosophy, it has not acquired a generally accepted meaning in either economic or juridical thought, and it certainly cannot be regarded as a technical term of art in international economic relations. Yet there is no doubt that the concept of the just price (as well as the closely related notion of a just relationship of prices) expresses political demands that are of considerable importance to the development of new international legal and institutional arrangements. It is particularly interesting to note that the concept which has long played a leading role in the grievances of the poor countries has recently received emphasis in the statements of spokesmen for the industrialized countries faced with the soaring prices of oil and minerals.[2] To some the idea of linking justice to prices may seem a vain effort to mingle ethical and economic factors (possibly with overtones of medieval metaphysics), but the political realities cannot be wished away, and the demands for fairness and equity in international pricing will have to be faced.

This is not to say that pricing patterns will be determined by abstract considerations of justice or that economic strength will become a minor factor in fixing prices. Obviously, governments and companies will continue to seek to maximize their benefits by taking advantage of strong positions and yielding when their positions are weak. Important as this is, it does not exclude the role of noneconomic factors, particularly as they affect the attitudes and positions of governments in undertaking collaboration and collective action. For one thing, the governments' perceptions of injustice as to economic returns generate tensions and demands which lead to political intervention on both the national and international levels. On the latter level, the necessity to win the acceptance of states with diverse interests tends to increase the importance of noneconomic factors and, particularly in recent times, the demand for more equitable distribution of goods in world trade.

It does not seem idle, therefore, to seek to clarify the conceptions of just prices which appear to be held by government spokesmen in international bodies. I shall attempt to do this largely on the basis of the debates in United Nations bodies which have focused mainly on the demands of developing countries for a larger share in world trade and on the consequences of rapidly rising prices of raw materials in world trade. In the light of these debates (principally in 1974), we can perceive some of the principal ideas underlying the conception of just prices and their practical implications.

In this analysis, it will be apparent that ideas of a fair price are largely addressed to specific and well-known grievances and that in the political debates little effort is made to formulate definitions of a theoretical kind. However, definitions are implicit in the arguments and it may help to clarify the issues by distinguishing the various senses in which the conception of just price is employed.

One such sense of the term is, of course, the classic economists' notion of the market price based on free trade and comparative advantage. (This, interestingly, is similar to the dominant medieval notion of the just price as one reached through free bargaining and full knowledge.) [3] Within international bodies this conception receives implicit support in the attack made on restrictive practices and monopolistic or oligopolistic conditions. A widely held thesis is that the international pricing of industrial products involves collusive practices, based on cartel arrangements and multinational company practices in restraint of free competition.[4] In contrast, it is maintained that agricultural products and raw materials are marketed under conditions of nearly perfect competition and often face discrimination in the markets of the industrialized world.[5] As we shall note later, recent developments involving petroleum and minerals have altered this thesis in some respects and have raised the issue of restraints on trade in an entirely different political context. However, the principal thrust against "monopolistic" and collusive arrangements is directed toward industrial goods rather than primary products and against the private sector rather than governments. The pricing and restrictive agreements made by the governments of countries producing raw materials have been justified by most of the developing countries as necessary defensive measures which help to achieve a more equitable balance in the terms of trade.[6]

A somewhat related but more complex proposition asserts that the structural features of the world economy tend toward a deterioration in the terms of trade against primary producers.[7] (The terms of trade can be summarized as the index of the average price of a country's exports in terms of the average price of its imports.) The gist of this analysis is that capital and technology are relatively scarce and therefore command an increasing economic rent which redounds to the benefit of the industrialized countries, whereas the producers of agricultural goods and raw materials face competitive conditions and inelastic demand. Whether or not there has been a long-run downward trend in terms of trade of the primary products is a matter of controversy among economists.[8] Bodies of the United Nations have continued to treat the proposition as amply confirmed, though some historical studies and the rise in commodity prices in the past decade tend to throw doubt on its validity.[9] Even so, it seems clear that at least in recent years many of the less-developed countries have been adversely affected by high costs in the food, fertilizers, and manufactures which they import from the developed countries. This is especially evident for the large group of countries with insufficient resources or with highly unfavorable demographic conditions (as in the Indian subcontinent) who have been severely prejudiced by such rising import prices without any equivalent rise in their own export prices.[10] These current trends in price relationship, which are particularly injurious to many, though not all, poor countries, have an important bearing on the complex idea of a just relationship between the prices of goods bought and the prices of those sold.

They support the conclusion that just prices cannot be equated with market prices, and that in many situations the desirable objective of an equitable relationship between the prices of goods sold and bought can only be achieved by manipulating prices for the benefit of the less-developed countries or by providing for other compensatory arrangements. As indicated in recent resolutions, this seems quite clearly to be the position adopted by the United Nations.[11] It is not, of course, inconsistent with the view that monopolistic restraints and restrictive business practices should be eliminated, but it clearly implies a conception of the just price that is different from the ideal market price. In this conception, just price might be defined as the price necessary to cover the costs of production, including the social costs of minimum welfare and development. The practical implication of this position in the present international situation is that concessionary arrangements, through prices or otherwise, are necessary to bring about equitable price relationships for the poorer countries. In effect, this means a one-way transfer of resources to the poor countries and therefore subsumes the case for just prices under the general principle of responsibility to assist the more needy countries. Under that principle, the requirement of concessionary arrangements or direct aid should be applicable not

only to industrialized countries but to some nonindus-
trialized resource-rich countries which sell vital resources to
the poor countries at relatively high prices.[12]

This last observation leads us to the highly controversial problem of just and fair prices for natural resource
products, notably petroleum, natural gas, and minerals,
which enjoy a strong market position and have had spectac-
ular price increases in the last few years. Not all raw materials are in this category, and the weaker primary products
present different problems of international pricing. However, as we shall suggest below, international solutions may
require action on a range of commodities to obtain general
acceptance and to achieve the objective of a just relationship
between prices. Before discussing such solutions, I shall
briefly summarize the issues of equity and justice that have
been raised by the price rises of the strong commodities in
the field of natural resources. My present concern with equity and justice does not, of course, imply that I consider
the market and other economic factors (and, in some respects, political power) as of lesser importance. These factors certainly set the critical limits for choices. But it is also
true that ethical and social values are involved, and that attitudes as to what is equitable may influence those choices.

As seen by the producing countries, the equitable justification for increasing the prices of their natural resource
products rests on several grounds, ranging from the moral
debt for past exploitation to the obligation to meet the
needs of future generations. What might be called the historical argument maintains that for several decades the importing countries, through coercion, had set prices at so low
a figure that they usurped the lion's share of the economic
rent of the natural resource. With the recent change in relative strength, arising from a combination of political, economic, and technological factors, the producing countries

have been able to reverse the situation and obtain redress for past exploitation.[13] In their view, to have refrained from the exercise of their economic power would have been to perpetuate the unjust relationship of the past. An answer to this line of argument (particularly as expressed by the companies and consumers in the purchasing countries) is that the technology and capital brought in by the importing countries made exploration and production possible and, therefore, the importing countries are entitled to a commensurate share of the economic rent.[14] The issue thus joined has generated considerable emotion and rhetoric, though neither leads to any new solutions. As we shall see, the other equitable issues appear to be more suggestive of constructive action.

A second equitable justification advanced by the producers is that they have been faced with the rapidly rising costs of imported goods and were thus entitled, on the basis of increased demand, to raise their prices to keep pace with inflationary trends in industrial countries.[15] Although this line of reasoning has not been entirely persuasive to consumers who compared the soaring prices of oil with the lesser price increases of other goods, it has appealed to many of the poorer countries which have been especially hard hit by increases in the import costs of manufactures, fertilizers, grains, and other commodities. The argument has served to underline the importance of a balanced movement in price relationships and the linkages between various commodities. These factors have emerged as significant elements in the efforts for new international measures.

A third line of justification put forward by the producers of petroleum and some minerals is that the high prices operate to bring about a more rational use and allocation of relatively scarce energy resources, both for present and future generations.[16] This thesis has cogency, particularly in light of the rapidly growing demands for energy and the consequential needs to expand existing resources and to create feasible new sources. Without entering into the statistical data, there is good reason to believe that a relatively high plateau of prices will not only further more rational and less wasteful consumption but also will almost certainly result in an appreciable acceleration of research, exploration, and development of conventional and novel sources of energy.[17] While this third line may be regarded as an economic justification, it also has an important element of equity since the welfare of disadvantaged peoples (as well as the unborn) requires the growth of productive capacity on a massive scale, and this need may be accorded a higher priority in terms of justice than the losses involved in short-term dislocations and higher prices to consumers in affluent countries.

There are, of course, arguments of an equitable character against the price increases. As we have already noted, those increases have caused severe deprivations for many disadvantaged countries, the most serious deprivations affecting fertilizer production and, in consequence, food supply.[18] This has been a widely recognized inequity of the sudden increase in oil prices, and remedial measures have been undertaken but remain inadequate. A two-tier pricing system (with lower prices for the most disadvantaged countries) has not been acceptable to producers (nor commended by economists), and it seems clear that the relief must be sought through direct assistance and investments rather than through discriminatory pricing.[19]

Industrialized countries have also argued that the scale of oil price rises has produced a substantial risk of worldwide depression which could have devastating consequences for nearly all countries, including the petroleum-producing countries.[20] Both the inflationary effect (adding to other

forces) of the oil price rises and the adverse consequences
they have produced on the balance of payments of importing countries brought about defensive measures that tended
to reduce world trade, create massive unemployment,
and lower production. Although these are economic
effects, they present questions as to the equities in bearing the costs and sacrifices that are involved in meeting
the problems. The petroleum-producing countries have ac-
knowledged their self-interest in avoiding a depression and
have stressed the benefits that would result from their recy-
cling enlarged funds to productive use in their own and
other countries.[21] International emergency programs for
the poor countries and for the especially disadvantaged industrialized countries have been proposed and undertaken,
but thus far on a relatively modest scale and less than adequate to meet the requirements. Some hope for more posi-
tive action may be found in the increased awareness in both
rich and poor countries that inflation and recession endan-
ger their social order and that the worldwide network of in-
terdependencies demands international solutions. There is,
also, a greater recognition of the fact that if international
solutions are to be generally acceptable considerations of
justice and equity as well as economic requirements must be
met.

Some such international measures have already been
alluded to in the previous comments, but it may be appropriate to indicate briefly the principal lines of approach
which seem feasible for international action in the near future. It will be seen that the measures suggested all involve
the application or development of legal concepts and principles and the creation of new international procedures for
their implementation.

One line of action would be the application of con-
certed measures to eliminate or reduce restrictive practices

by companies and cartels, whether private or public. It will be recalled that an effort of that kind aborted in the still-born Havana Charter of 1948.[22] In recent years, however, renewed attempts have been made under the United Nations to identify the undesirable practices (such as territorial allocations, restrictive licensing provisions, transfer pricing policies, and cartel arrangements) which have had significantly adverse effects for developing countries, and these efforts suggest the need for international guidelines and possibly eventually for a code of impermissible practices.[23] Presumably, implementation would have to be left largely to national legislation and enforcement, but these actions might be supplemented by international inquiry and consultation procedures. The concern over multinational companies and the recent developments in regional groups (such as the European Economic Community and the Andean group) tend to encourage the emergence of a new political consensus in favor of continued international effort against restrictive practices. Although the producers' associations in the developing countries fall into a special category and are strongly supported within the international bodies, suggestions have been made by various countries in both the developed and developing world that these associations should also conform to international standards directed against restraints on supply and trade of a discriminatory character.[24] There is reason to believe that this could more readily be achieved through separate arrangements on a commodity basis than through general rules, but the acceptability of particular arrangements would be influenced not only by the specific quid pro quos by both sides but also, in some degree, by the general climate of opinion manifested in principles relating to restrictive and oligopolistic practices. The subject calls for extensive international study and consultation.

A second category of measures would comprise the

multilateral commodity arrangements which are aimed at achieving stability for a particular commodity or perhaps a class of related commodities. Such commodity arrangements have traditionally been addressed to situations of price instability which were particularly hard on the producers of primary commodities.[25] No doubt it is still easier to begin with these weak commodities. However, even for the strong commodities, high prices and interruptions in supply tend to make it economically feasible for buyers to exploit alternative sources and also for producers to expand the scale of production of the commodity in question or of substitutes for it. As a consequence, countries producing some strong commodities might gain from international arrangements which would be directed toward slowing the upward trend of the development of new sources and the downward trend in the need for old sources. Apart from this factor, both sides have an interest in smoothing out those heights and depths in commodity prices and production which affect all producers and consumers and in coming to an arrangement which would achieve a flexible adaptation to supply and demand.[26] International market regulation for these purposes requires a set of procedures for exchange of information and consultation on conditions which determine the price of the commodity in question (as, for example, supply and demand, stocks and reserves, replacement costs, and feasibility of replacement). It would also require agreement on the procedures for negotiations based, to the extent possible, on agreed criteria for assuring a flow of supply and a reasonable return to producers. In some cases, buffer stocks may be a critical feature of the arrangement. Under commodity agreements with adequate information on market conditions and costs available to both sides, a negotiated price might be as close to a "just" price as one could expect in international trade.

These comments may well seem optimistic to economists who are sceptical about attempts to regulate international commodity markets and to officials who are aware of the difficulties of obtaining agreement and compliance by governments to controls which appear to be contrary to their immediate economic interest. Their misgivings can be justified by the history of commodity agreements. Only a handful of significant economic agreements have been concluded (concerning the commodities coffee, cocoa, sugar, wheat, and tin) and only one, tin, may be said to have worked with some effectiveness. Moreover, it is not difficult to point out how such agreements have led to distortions and rigidities that were inimical to long-run considerations. On the other hand, it is evident that most governments, developed as well as developing, are now deeply concerned about extreme price fluctuations and the need for adequate and secure supplies. As a consequence, the idea of commodity arrangements, with export quotas and buffer stocks, has won a wider degree of support. Even a country as committed to a free market as the United States has moved toward a selective commodity agreement approach that would increase price stability and assist the developing countries in their export earnings.[27]

One central point of difference between the developed and developing countries is that the former, the industrialized countries, generally favor a selective approach commodity by commodity and lay stress on the special characteristics of each commodity. In contrast, the developing countries tend toward a comprehensive set of arrangements covering all or many commodities. An important manifestation of this has been the so-called "integrated approach" proposed in UNCTAD by the developing countries. The essence of that scheme is the establishment of an internationally financed stockpile of a wide range of commodities (eighteen are suggested in the UNCTAD proposal), together with a series of commitments for sales and purchases, plus compensatory financing, local processing, and the removal of discriminatory barriers to processed products.[28] Thus the strategy of the scheme is the creation of a community of interest among the participants by including various commodities (so that countries will in some cases be producers and in other cases consumers). As proposed, the scheme also has a multidimensional character; it would provide for expanded access to markets and for measures of diversification in the production and security of supplies. While the scheme has considerable appeal because of its wide-ranging character, it has encountered some opposition from developed countries concerned over the rigidities that may be introduced in the world market. Moreover, producer countries may suffer from price stabilization: since they could not compensate for shortages in production due to natural causes, their income would be reduced. In addition, operating an international buffer stock for eighteen diverse commodities is a costly and difficult undertaking for international organs.[29] Despite these problems, the conception of the comprehensive integrated approach is likely to remain an important focal point in the continuing international negotiations directed toward bringing more stability into world markets.

The impact of inflation on the poorer countries has given impetus to proposals for an international price-indexing system under which increases in the prices of goods imported into the poor countries would be matched by increases in their export prices. In effect, this would constitute an extension to the international level of such national techniques as parity-pricing schemes in agriculture and cost-of-living clauses in wage contracts. Ideally, a general system of price indexation should be attractive to both developed and developing countries particularly in the light of widespread inflation, but under present political and economic conditions its practical implementation on a world scale is a formidable undertaking. Indexation may, however, prove viable for a limited number of commodities in world trade.[30] They would probably have to be commodities whose supply could be controlled as, for example, by buffer stocks, production regulation, or export controls, depending on the particular commodity. Such supply control can be more easily achieved for commodities with relatively inelastic price demand. International commodity agreements would be the preferred instruments for indexation arrangements, but in some cases long-term contracts and producers' associations might also be used. Proponents of indexing claim that by reducing short-term instability of prices, indexing could bring about an improved international allocation of resources and might lead to a more economical use of nonrenewable resources. It has also been noted that indexation of primary commodity prices may provide a stimulus to the developed market countries to reduce their rates of domestic inflation since the prices of their commodity imports would decline as a result of reductions in the prices of their export goods.

The drawbacks of international indexation—both technical and economic—should not, however, be overlooked. The rigidities introduced by an automatic link between the price of particular commodities to manufactured goods prices (or any other indicator of purchasing power) is likely to bring about an inefficient allocation of resources and may invite the substitution of products to the detriment of the producers. Moreover, since most trading is not done on a government to government basis, elaborate arrangements would be required on the part of all the main trading countries to impose indexing in trade contracts. Another difficulty would be determining the starting date, or reference date, of an indexation scheme, since commodities do not peak at the same time or fluctuate in similar ways.[31] For this and other reasons, indexation could have highly unequal and inequitable effects as between producers as well as consumers. It is not at all clear that governments would be able to iron out the technical difficulties and accept the economic consequences of a wide-ranging indexation arrangement. However, limited indexation agreements in long-range supply contracts for particular commodities are likely to become more common.

A more acceptable approach to the problem of commodity fluctuations is an export earnings stabilization arrangement. Such an arrangement would not fix prices but would increase the stability of the export earnings of developing countries through compensatory payments for short-falls in their earnings. Such schemes have been described as "passive" or "indirect" indexation and as necessary supplements to price stabilization. However, the stabilization of earnings can be and actually is being carried out independent of indexing or commodity price regulation. One such scheme is operated by the International Monetary Fund. It provides for automatic compensation for shortfalls of export earnings of a short-term character and requires repayment. Another scheme, known as STABEX, was established at the Lomé Convention of 1975 between the European Economic Community and forty-six countries in Africa, the Caribbean, and the Pacific regions (ACP). The essence of that scheme is the compensation of exporting countries when, through no fault of their own, their earnings from exports to the EEC fall below the normal levels. The scheme applies to export receipts from a specified number of commodities rather than to total export earnings (as under the IMF scheme). Most of the beneficiary countries (the neediest) are exempt from any repayment obligation, and the others only have to repay transfers in special circumstances of price rises. Although these two schemes are limited in their application, they are likely to be the forerunners of more comprehensive efforts.

In comparison to indexation or commodity price regulation, there are definite advantages to an export earnings stabilization arrangement. It is more specifically linked to the needs of individual countries, and it can benefit the producers suffering from temporary disruptions in production. As we observed earlier, the stabilization of prices, in contrast, would reduce producers' earnings when natural disasters or interruptions in production cut their output. Another advantage of an earnings scheme is that if a country is heavily dependent on more than one export commodity, some of which may not be suitable for commodity agreements, an earnings stabilization scheme linked to many or all exports will provide more effective assistance. Consumer countries would benefit since they would probably have a higher level of exports to the producer countries receiving compensation than would otherwise be the case. Moreover, they would have a reduced risk of future supply shortages because producer countries would be enabled to maintain their investment in productive capacity. In the light of these advantages, it is to be expected that new arrangements for comprehensive export earnings stabilization will be developed and put into effect.[32]

If we look beyond the various technical schemes relating to raw material prices, what conclusions may be drawn from the present trends about the main issues of distributive justice? One conclusion, clearly, is that the "free" market system is widely regarded as inadequate to assure "stable, remunerative and equitable prices" for most raw material exports of the developing countries. Although this proposition may seem to have been evident for a long time, it has only recently been accepted on a wide scale by the major market-economy countries in the developed world. The positions taken by the United States, Britain, and France (referred to above) are a significant indication that the classic principles of free trade will be substantially modified by the "interventionist" commodity arrangements which are now emerging. The dissenting voices of some economists and a few governments (notably, the West German and Japanese) are not likely to deflect this trend. The moral case in favor of intervention neatly summarized in the statement of the French foreign minister that "the forces of the market place are blind and merciless to the weak" has been supported by the widespread belief that the disparities in economic power among nations destroy the raison d'être of the market as an instrument of optimum allocation.

It has, of course, been pointed out that the responses of the industrialized countries to demands for commodity price support are not entirely attributable to moral factors. They also reflect the vulnerability of these countries to the strengthened position of the producers of oil and some minerals and, more generally, the political need to ease tensions and to avoid confrontation. An even more specific assertion of their self-interest is the observation that the industrialized countries produce "some seventy percent of the world's food and raw materials, and accounting for a third of world trade in these commodities they do not wish to see prices tumble." [33]

It can hardly be denied that all of these factors of self-interest have played a role in bringing about concessions to the demands of the raw material producing countries. This does not mean, however, that the outcome cannot be judged in accordance with criteria of equity. As we have noted before, self-interest as a motivating force does not exclude a result which should be regarded as equitable because it meets pressing needs and legitimate expectations. On that basis, it is apparent that the schemes for commodity arrangements will be widely perceived as steps toward greater equity.

It is important, however, to recognize that stabilization of raw material prices and preferential treatment for producer countries may not go very far in remedying the basic conditions which give rise to unequal bargaining relations. The crucial fact is that countries which are highly dependent on one or two raw materials (with the notable exception of oil) are at a continuing disadvantage in their economic relations with the industrialized countries. This is especially true where the relevant raw materials face the threat of substitutes, whether natural or synthetic, or where they are otherwise "weak" commodities in world markets. It has been trenchantly observed, for example, that there is little sense in the developing countries' use of their best lands to grow tropical products which are "a drag on the market" most of the time in a period when there is a highly favorable market for cereals, livestock, and feed. Similarly, it has been observed that the industrialization of developing countries has often meant acquiring the most highly competitive industries which have markets that are rapidly saturated. The thrust of these comments is that only through a substantial redeployment of industrial capacity (a "new international division of labor") and far-reaching reforms in agricultural production will most of the poor developing countries be able to attain sufficient strength to produce greater equality in their bargaining relations. To this end, considerable rhetorical emphasis is now being placed on "self-reliance" and on cooperation among developing countries themselves, rather than on concessions and aid from the industrialized countries. Attractive as this strategy of self-help may appear to countries desperately anxious to free themselves from dependence on the rich countries, the strategy cannot be a substitute for the technology and capital as well as the markets which are available in the industrialized world. For this reason, international acceptance of price stabilization schemes and compensatory financing remains important, not only to furnish a needed element of economic security but also as an indirect means of transferring resources to countries in need. However, for the more fundamental remedies, the acquisition of technology, the development of natural resources, and the restructuring of agriculture must be the principal objectives. We shall now turn to these subjects.

Sharing Technology

The idea that knowledge is a collective good which should be freely available across national lines has a powerful appeal and is often taken as axiomatic. We find it formulated as a principle in international declarations [34] and as a justification for the dissemination of scientific and technological knowledge throughout the world. But the principle has a deceptive simplicity. The complexities become evident when we consider the demands for the transfer of technology from those countries which possess it to those which seek it. That these demands are strongly advanced comes as no surprise. It is increasingly obvious that technology is the critical factor in the exploitation of resources and in industrial and agricultural production; without it most countries are condemned to penury and stagnation. The acuteness of the needs and the sense of entitlement to a share in the collective pool of human knowledge combine to create a strong political and intellectual movement for the more effective transmittal of technology to the poor and less-developed countries.

Complications arise because technological knowledge is only, in a partial sense, a collective good. A large part of it especially relevant to economic development is proprietary, regarded in law and in fact as property, representing the fruits of investment and effort. This includes product design, processes, and managerial and engineering know-how. Much of this technology is owned by enterprises (whether or not patented) which treat technology as a commodity to be sold, although it is often, unlike other commodities, not freely available in open markets. This is not simply due to ill will or greed. The constraints on such availability are deeply imbedded in the economic and legal conditions that govern the operation of such enterprises and are not easily dissolved. Apart from the proprietary character of technology, there is still another more deep-seated reason why science and technology cannot simply be regarded as a common pool of knowledge readily utilizable by all countries having access to it. This reason, in gist, is the complex barrier resulting from disparities which often exist between donor and recipient in respect to social systems, values, education, skills, and other imponderables which affect the selection and employment of imported technology. These disparities give rise to constraints and frustrations that run through the process of transfer. They affect both donors and recipients, and they are not easily overcome by institutional mechanisms or beneficent attitudes.

In pointing out these complications, I do not wish to suggest that the idea of scientific and technological knowledge as a common pool to be used for the benefit of all is entirely invalid or without practical significance. It has, indeed, a valid application to the large body of scientific and technical knowledge in the public domain and even to the use of proprietary technology. Its acceptance as a general principle provides a basis for international efforts to disseminate such knowledge and to overcome some of the constraints imposed by the conditions described above. On the other hand, one must bear in mind that in many situations an insistence on free and unrestricted availability could impede actual transfer or adversely affect the effective utilization of technology. This will become apparent as we analyze the problems of transfer.

From the standpoint of our theme of the equitable sharing of resources, it is of particular interest to consider three problems of acute concern to the developing countries:

(1), the restrictive practices of suppliers of technology and their impact on national autonomy with respect to production and distribution;

(2), the deficiencies in the bargaining process between the suppliers of technology and the developing countries, especially when the latter are faced with the quasi-monopolistic power of transnational companies;

(3), the problem of reallocating a greater share of productive capacity to the less-developed countries in the interests of equity and economic rationality.

While recognizing that each of these problems involves a considerable degree of economic and political complexity, my comments will be addressed mainly to the normative and institutional proposals that have been made to meet them.

Most poor countries in need of imported technology have good reason to regard themselves as seriously handicapped in bargaining with large, foreign suppliers of technology. Their sense of weakness results not only from an awareness of their need and dependency and the quasi-

monopolistic position of suppliers, but also from the complexity of the choices to be made and their lack of knowledge of the consequences of various alternatives. In almost
every case, numerous elements are involved in a transfer
bargaining transaction, and the trade-offs among them are
not easy to evaluate.[35] There is a need to take into account
both the specific terms of a transfer (price, quality, etc.) and
general economic policies, social costs, and welfare considerations. Such social costs are often a consequence of restrictive provisions demanded by foreign suppliers (e.g.,
restrictions on exports and on production), and they may
also result from the "inappropriate" use of capital intensive
technology when labor is abundant and more employment
is desired. Choices are complicated because a proposed arrangement cannot be evaluated by itself; it needs to be compared with possible alternative arrangements and with the
"opportunity costs" involved in foregoing other uses of resources. The appraisal must be far wider than a cost-benefit
analysis which is limited to explicit quantifiable elements
such as royalties, direct employment effects, and foreign
exchange costs, leaving the rest to *ceteris paribus* assumptions. In the words of a Latin American expert "What is
needed is not an analysis in *ceteris paribus* terms but a con-
ceptualization of the problem as a whole to identify the *ceteris.*"[36]

The principal factors with which developing countries
are concerned in appraising alternative transfer mechanisms include:[37]

(a), profits, royalties, or fees to be paid;

(b), conditions imposed by suppliers (such as transfer
pricing, restrictive provisions, and duration of licensing
contracts);

(c), the "unpackaging" of proposed transfers—that is,
the ability to obtain required inputs of technology, capital,

management, export links, and the like separately rather than in a package;

(d), national control, including noneconomic objectives (e.g., employment, taxation, and development policies);

(e), the benefits to be obtained from the training of indigenous personnel and development of national technological and industrial capability outside of the firm.

Each one of these major factors is greatly affected by the restrictive conditions imposed by the suppliers of technology in most commercial transfers of technology. This is a pervasive problem which raises issues of equity, power, and efficiency. The fact that most technology is proprietary and sold by business enterprises in an imperfect market, often under quasi-monopolistic conditions, has resulted in a wide range of practices designed to restrict competition and protect the position of the supplier. They occur not only in transactions with developing countries but also within and between industrialized countries, some of which have long endeavored to control such practices through national legislation. However, the problems are aggravated when transfers are made by large companies from the industrialized areas to the developing countries. The disparities in bargaining power and the dependency of the developing countries give rise to an acute sense of inequity and an inability to resist onerous and discriminatory practices. The sellers of technology cannot be compelled to make transfers on terms unacceptable to them, and when the purchasers lack economic strength, their efforts to eliminate restrictive provisions may prevent the transaction entirely. That is why, for example, Japan is in a position to insist on conditions for imported technology which most economically weaker countries cannot demand without losing the transfer.

One way of meeting the problem is to develop an effective common front among recipients so that suppliers will not find markets for their technology on their restrictive terms. Efforts to this end include, among other things, the common adoption of national regulatory measures whereby undesirable practices are outlawed or controlled by national authorities and which, if widely accepted by recipient countries, would substantially reduce the ability of the transnational companies to impose restrictive terms. In addition, attempts have been made in regional groups to adopt common regulations against restrictive practices. The effectiveness of such regulations would depend on the economic strength and attractiveness of the combined economic union, as is the case for the European Economic Community. In the developing world, the Cartagena Treaty of the Andean countries provides the leading example of a well-conceived regulatory scheme (expressed in its Decision 24) though its actual impact is not yet clear.[38] Beyond these efforts, there is a movement for a universal code of conduct that would eliminate and regulate undesirable restrictive practices. An attempt to do this was made as far back as 1948 in the aborted Havana Charter for an International Trade Organization and a few years ago in a United Nations effort to draft a restrictive business practices convention. In recent years, the strong political position of the developing countries and their increased concern over the inequities and abuses of restrictive provisions in technology transfers have intensified the efforts for international regulation through a code or a legally binding treaty.[39] To appreciate the scope and complexity of this proposed code, one must realize how extensive a range of common practices would be regulated. They can conveniently be divided into five categories.[40]

One such category includes the cartellike arrangements among suppliers of technology which impose limitations on the market for would-be purchasers. Such collusive arrangements through diverse associations and suppliers' agreements result in the allocation of territories, restriction of sales, limitation of production, fixing prices and terms of sale, and similar measures which have the result of placing barriers to the acquisition of technology by developing countries on reasonable competitive terms.

A second category of restrictive practices involves the more direct imposition of limitations on purchasers in their use and production of the technology. A common example is a restriction on the "field of use," as by barring a recipient from using a technique to make products of a different kind. Another frequent restriction prohibits the purchase of competitive technology. There are often clauses under which patent and trademark licences cannot be assigned or sublicenced. The volume of production may be limited, irrespective of needs or demands. An especially abusive practice involves forcing a recipient to acquire technologies that he does not want because of the packaging requirement.

A third category—one that has received much international attention—relates to restrictions on the distribution of products, particularly export restrictions. Such restrictions are often explicit in technology contracts which impose total or partial prohibitions on exports of products resulting from the imported technology. Not infrequently, export restrictions are indirect, as, for example, when parent companies supplying the technology exercise managerial control over the exports of a subsidiary or affiliate in the developing country. The not uncommon use of export limitations to protect the market position of the supplier has aroused much adverse criticism, but it has been difficult to eliminate, even when forbidden by law. There is no doubt that such export restrictions run counter to competitive trade principles, and that they also impede regional economic cooperation and the growth of marketing capability in the developing countries. But many suppliers of technology are reluctant to make technology available to a country if the result will be to reduce their markets in other countries. Hence a recipient country is often faced with a take it or leave it proposition involving a no export clause.

Still another category of restrictive practices relates to hidden costs and pricing policies. The most prominent of these are tie-in arrangements requiring payments for related goods and services which may not be wanted at all or which are sold only at noncompetitive prices. This is why there is an insistent demand by developing countries for the disaggregation or unpackaging of the technology transfer and for the itemization of separate costs. Another controversial aspect involving hidden costs consists of the transfer prices charged by parent companies for goods and services "sold" to their subsidiaries in the developing countries in connection with the technology. Such transfer prices can be manipulated in order to lower apparent profits and to avoid taxes or national controls. It is charged that they are often higher than market or "arms-length" prices and that they impose excessive costs on the poorer countries. Efforts to deal with this by national legislation have had very limited effects.

In a fifth category of restrictive practices I would include the variety of limitations on the development of the capabilities of the purchasers and the recipient countries. These are especially resented as unfair and abusive. For example, many technology transfer arrangements prohibit a recipient to undertake his own research and technical development or to make changes in the technology purchased. Another oft-cited example is the "grant-back" requirement under which the purchaser is required to pass on to the supplier, often free of charge, any improvements that may be made. These grant-backs are particularly resented when they are nonreciprocal (without any equivalent benefit to recipient) and exclusive, that is, when the supplier alone has the rights to improvements made by the recipient. An opposite provision, but one also objectionable to the purchaser, is the requirement that he must buy all future improvements in the technology. Still another grievance results from requirements that key managerial and technical positions be reserved for personnel of the supplier even if indigenous alternative personnel are available. A strong response to this type of restriction is found in the legislation of many countries which impose limits on expatriate staff and require local managerial appointments and the training of local personnel.

As I have already noted, there is a strong feeling among developing countries that restrictive practices of the kind just summarized should be outlawed or controlled by international regulatory action as well as by national legislation. The aim of an international code, whether binding or not, would be to promote national legislative and administrative measures and, where appropriate, regional conventions that would apply reasonably uniform standards in order to eliminate or control undesirable practices. A difference of view exists between the industrialized countries, which tend to favor a nonbinding code or guidelines, and the developing countries, which favor a legally mandatory treaty. However, since ratification by the developed countries is not thought likely in the near future, the conception of a body of rules that would be binding on those who accept it as such but only a guide to those who do not has emerged as an intermediary compromise that may prove acceptable.[41] There are various other divergences between the positions of industrialized and developing countries. The former are concerned over a tendency to impose obligations solely on the suppliers of technology, and they urge that these obligations be balanced by requiring fair treatment for suppliers from recipients (by, for example, imposing a duty to maintain quality standards, providing for appropriate market protection, and assuring impartial arbitration of disputes). Another contentious question is whether rules against restrictive practices should be categorical and specific or whether they should be somewhat general and allow for exceptions (a "rule of reason"). The implementation and enforcement of a code, even if binding, is generally considered to be the province of national authorities. However, there is wide support for international inquiry, monitoring, and discussion as supplementary means of bringing about compliance.

The widespread acceptance of a code and the adoption of effective national regulation to eliminate or control restrictive practices would, on the whole, strengthen the bargaining position of the developing countries. This would be primarily a consequence of a common front of recipients, greatly reducing the options of the suppliers to find markets in weaker or more tractable countries. In addition, the ability of officials of the developing countries to bargain and to resist pressures tends to be enhanced when national and international regulation prohibits certain restrictive practices or imposes controls. But one must also bear in mind that if the economic position is weak, standards may be set too high, so that suppliers will withhold their technology.

To meet this, measures are required to improve the economic position and negotiating strength of the developing countries. One such measure is the creation of larger markets through regional integration or similar arrangements. This has been one of the objectives of the Andean group and of other economic regional arrangements which hope to follow the successful experience of the European Common Market in attracting outside technology.[42] Secondly, an enhancement of technological capability may be achieved through research and development institutions and through intergovernmental organs which provide advice and knowledge. It is highly probable that the regional arrangements for this purpose, now still embryonic and experimental, will be strengthened and that new arrangements will be made for regional groupings which now lack them.

The advantages of pooling knowledge are but an aspect of the larger issue of the relation of knowledge to bargaining strength. In classic economic theory, it is assumed that adequate information is available for competitive market relations. Under the imperfect market conditions in which technology is transferred to developing countries, knowledge is a critical element in the bargaining power of both parties, but generally the developing country is disadvantaged since it lacks the scientific and technical infrastructure in the public sector for applied research and development. What the developing country needs are institutes for technological research, resource surveys, labor productivity and market surveys, engineering data, and a variety of other tasks relevant to the economic and social use of technology. However, it must be noted that while no one doubts the utility of such research activity, there is some scepticism as to its practical value for technology transfer. In large part, this scepticism arises from the gap in effective communication between scientific institutes and government bureaus or businessmen.[43] There are also deficiencies in qualified personnel and material support which limit the effectiveness of national institutes. To compensate for these shortcomings, regional efforts have been encouraged, as have global international institutes. Moreover, in several cases the industrialized countries have created programs specially directed to so-called "adaptive research" in the applicability of new techniques to the less-developed countries. The most successful efforts have occurred in the agricultural sector through such organizations as the International Rice Institute and the centers concerned with tropical agriculture. There is clearly a need for a worldwide structure for the acquisition and dissemination of technical knowledge with extensive interlinkages between global, regional, and national centers. It should promote close connections between the universities and scientific institutes on the one side and the enterprises, both public and private, concerned with the practical adoption and use of technology. The new United Nations University may have a significant contribution to make in this regard.

Some other ideas for the spread of knowledge and intelligence have a sharper edge to them. One of these is based on the premise that the disclosure of business and technical information relating to transfer arrangements would be of great value to the would-be purchasers of such technology in the developing countries. Generally, agreements for the purchase of technology are kept secret. Foreign companies regard it as in their interest to maintain such secrecy, as do most recipient governments in regard to contracts of their nationals and purchases by public bodies. It has been pointed out that this may not be in the interest of developing countries since a policy of secrecy reduces their strength by segmenting information and "accentuating problems of relative ignorance." [44] One proposal is that disclosure should be made a matter of international or regional public policy under which recipient governments would exchange information about practices and the terms of purchases, and international bodies would assist in the dissemination of such information. There are obvious difficulties in the way of this proposal since the suppliers of technology are reluctant (as are many governments) to reveal terms which may be more favorable in some cases than in others. However, this was also true for concession agreements in the field of resource exploitation, and government policies in several countries have now brought about registration and public availability of such agreements. More important than that have been the arrangements among developing countries in producers' associations (led by OPEC) to disseminate information about their own arrangements to other producers. It has been suggested that a similar disclosure policy should be followed by the developing countries which have entered into agreements for the importation of technology.

Another proposal is that countries introduce the principle of the most favored nation clause into contracts and licenses for technology transfer.[45] Under this clause the supplier would agree to transfer technology on a non-discriminatory basis: if he grants more favorable terms to one country, he must do the same for all others. It has been noted that in some cases this has been done in respect to concession agreements and that it also has been followed by OPEC for its members. In regard to technology transfer, demands for a most favored contract clause by a group of recipient countries might be accepted by some suppliers facing a common front of potential purchasers. The recipients would presumably benefit in situations where negotiations take place at different times. Whether this can be achieved depends on the cohesion of the recipient group and its relative strength vis-à-vis particular suppliers. The "precedent" of OPEC and other mineral agreements may be misleading since here it is the suppliers of technology, not the purchasers, who are more like the producers of raw materials in their oligopolistic position and in their ability to exact quasi-rents for goods with a scarcity value to the user. But there could be situations in which suppliers would accept a most favored contract clause in order to obtain markets in a number of countries. For such clauses to be effective, the usual confidentiality of contracts and licenses would have to be modified so that the terms would be known to potential purchasers. There are also practical difficulties in making decisions about the relative value of the terms of a contract. Most contracts have a number of elements which are not easily compared as a package (e.g., high royalties for a short time against low royalties for a long duration). The context of an agreement is also difficult to compare with others: prices, market size, economic infrastructure, personnel availability all affect the value of a contract and therefore have to be considered when determining what terms are more favorable than others. In view of these problems of comparability and disclosure, the efficacy of most favored contract and license clauses would require a strong national regulatory administration with ample authority to take into account all the relevant terms of a contract and to obtain full information from the supplier.

I turn now from the problem of bargaining and the terms of technology transfers to the wider problem of action to increase the flow of technology to the developing world. Put in even more general terms, the objective, as defined by United Nations bodies, is to bring about a substantial redeployment of productive capacity in industry from the developed to the developing countries. In the United Nations Industrial Development Organization, a declaration was adopted which stated that by the year 2000 [46] the share of industrial production by the developing countries should be 25 percent of world production. In 1975 the share was roughly 7 percent. It is urged, particularly by the developing countries, that this international division of labor should be pursued through a restructuring of world industry and a massive transfer of technical resources and capital to the poorer countries. The principal instruments for this would be the public institutions of the developed countries and the new capital-exporting countries of the developing world (that is, the petroleum-producing countries with comparatively small populations) together with the international financing institutions.[47] Underlying this idealistic program is the assumption that the common interest of nearly all countries would be served by some kind of international planning process that would bring about a more rational allocation of productive capacity in accordance with the needs and factor endowment of various countries. The energy, mineral, and other raw material resources in the developing countries, and their abundant supply of less costly labor, and, on the other side, the capital-intensive technologies, expensive specialized labor, and environmental concerns of the industrialized countries are seen as a realistic foundation for a relocation of industry that would be in keeping with the classic principle of comparative advantage, even though carried out largely through public institutions assisted by international consultative, monitoring, and indicative planning mechanisms. It may be prudent to add that this optimistic outlook found in the programmatic reports of international bodies does not entirely subdue the scepticism of those who tend to be more conscious of the pressures of national interest and of the obstacles to centralized planning on a world scale.

Yet such natural and not unreasonable scepticism should not obscure from us the movement in the direction of a planned relocation of industry to the less-developed world that has actually taken place. We can observe this, first, in national developments which are just emerging; second, in regional and interregional arrangements; and last, in the global efforts of the United Nations.

The most interesting indications on the national level are found in certain developed countries (such as Japan, the Netherlands, and Sweden) which are beginning to take practical measures for a planned restructuring of their industry so as to eliminate certain types of production and assist in their relocation to developing countries. This is not so extraordinary since for some industries such relocation has already taken place in response to market forces, as illustrated by the shift of textile production from the United States and the United Kingdom to many of the less-developed countries. However, there is novelty in the conception of planned relocations backed by public institutions with capital flows, extensive technical advice to the developing countries, and adjustment assistance for those affected in the industrial country. Practical steps in this conception can be seen in action taken by the Netherlands.[48] There one institution has been established to concentrate on the domestic restructuring of industry, to examine particular industries in Holland, and to devise plans for phasing out operations. It would do this in close cooperation with labor unions and employers. A complementary institution has also been set up to assist in the transfer to developing countries of the capital, technology, and skills of the phased-out sectors that are required for industrial production in those countries. It is realized that to make this effective, there would also have to be a lowering of trade barriers for exports from the relocated industries in the developing countries, and that such action would require international coordination. Some questions as to practical implementation come to mind: for example, will developing countries take the integrated packages offered instead of seeking "unpackaged" technology, and will the industrialized countries generally agree to the removal of protective trade barriers? But, even while recognizing that there are problems of implementation, one should not underestimate the significance of the Netherlands example. It may point the way to the wider acceptance of national relocation programs which seek to anticipate economic and social changes through planning that takes into account various elements in the relocation process and combines governmental cooperation on the international level with cooperation among the affected groups within the domestic polity.

On the international level, the objective of a large-scale transfer of industry to the developing areas has not only received emphatic support in resolutions, but also it has been given more concrete form through the articulation of a comprehensive strategy of ways and means to achieve it. Two international instruments adopted in 1975 exhibit this: one is the Lima Declaration and Plan of Action adopted by near unanimity in the United Nations Industrial Development Organization (UNIDO); [49] the other is the Lomé Convention between the European Economic Community and forty-six developing countries in Africa, the Caribbean, and Pacific regions (ACP). [50] Both instruments show the extent to which industrial redeployment and the sharing of knowledge and skills are seen as part of a complex multifaceted whole in which numerous elements interact with each other and need to be fitted into a total strategy. The relocation of industry is placed in a wide context which includes resource exploitation, terms of trade, foreign investment, transnational companies, income distribution, social welfare, education, and many other factors. Although this may appear to be a repetition of numerous specific demands and grievances, the conception of a linked strategy has implications for normative and institutional action. It naturally leads to efforts to develop coherent normative models in which the diverse interacting elements would each play its part. This is not far from international planning, though at the present stage—and probably for a long time ahead—this must be seen in an intellectual and negotiating framework rather than as an exercise of centralized authority. As such, its practical effect is to widen the range of bargaining between states and to facilitate the taking of a longer-range view than would otherwise be the case. It also leads to a much greater emphasis on national and regional planning and, in consequence, to a greater reliance on regulation and supervision by governments rather than the allowance of an unrestricted play of market forces.

The adoption of a comprehensive strategy also tends to bring a greater emphasis on international monitoring and other "intelligence" activities. Both the Lomé Convention and the UNIDO Plan of Action call for informational exchanges, expanded research, and the systematic review and appraisal of efforts. The European Economic Community has made commitments in the Lomé Convention to furnish technological information, facilitate contacts between firms and the ACP countries, assist in expanding research facilities, and establish a center for these ends. Institutional steps are being taken in UNIDO for various informational activities, ranging from an "industrial and technological data bank" to a series of systematic "urgent" consultations between officials of industrialized and developing countries on the possibilities and conditions for redeployment of certain productive capacities.

It is true that the proliferation of proposals for information exchange, consultations, negotiation, and for industrial centers may create an impression of a rather formless profusion of bodies all discussing the same subject without any discernible impact on the actual movement of resources. There is almost a Kafka-like quality to the picture of endless meetings, consultations, and movement from place to place of experts unconnected with the real events involved in the transfer of technology and industry. But we should not allow this image to obscure either the effect of the dissemination of ideas or of the active promotion of the goal of redeployment by governmental and industrial experts. Their activity has a reality because it is part of the process of adjusting to changes in the world economy—epitomized by the new price level of energy—and to the consequential shifts in power. "The cards have been reshuffled," Mr. de Seynes has pointed out, "and where we used to rely solely on exhortation and moral suasion we now have the hope of a more genuine negotiation, a negotiation in which security and regularity of supplies of essential raw materials could be viewed within the broadest possible context of measures affecting trade, aid, investment, and technology." [51] The direction of that broad negotiation is indicated and, in some degree, influenced by the objectives laid down in the United Nations resolutions. For example, these resolutions envisage long-term agreements on product specialization and a corresponding allocation of production through industrial complementary agreements; they suggest international subcontracting arrangements; they indicate procedures to achieve industrial complementarity and to share experience in industrialization; they call for new joint enterprises in agro-industries, in marine transport, and other fields; they propose studying the revision of international conventions on patents and trademarks. These examples illustrate the movement from broad objectives to specific legal agreements and procedures for the many-sided process of relocation of industry. They are especially relevant to our central theme because they envisage the sharing of resources and production capacity to meet both "the imperatives of justice" for those in need and the common interest of all countries in a more stable and secure economic order.

Permanent Sovereignty
over Natural Resources

In recent years no normative principle has been more vigorously asserted by the less-developed countries than that of "permanent sovereignty over natural resources," a concept generally defined by its proponents as the "inalienable" right of each state to the full exercise of authority over its natural wealth and the correlative right to dispose of its resources fully and freely.[52] For many developing countries this right is regarded as an essential condition of their national independence and of their ability to decide on basic political and economic arrangements. The main thrust of the demand for permanent sovereignty, both in rhetoric and in practice, has been to justify either the nationalization of foreign firms or their transfer of ownership to nationals of the host countries, especially in the extractive industries. In its strong form, the principle is asserted to legitimize the refusal of states to submit to international standards or international tribunals disputes relating to nationalization or other takeovers.[53] In a somewhat weaker form, the concept of permanent sovereignty serves to provide justification for a variety of national measures which impose limits and duties on foreign firms, as, for example, requiring them to employ nationals of the country in managerial capacities, to meet local supply needs first, to give up repatriation of profits, and to renegotiate contracts prior to their agreed expiry.[54] On the international level, the principle of permanent sovereignty has become the focal normative conception used by states to justify their right to exercise control over production and distribution arrangements without being hampered by the international law of state responsibility as it had been traditionally interpreted by the capital-exporting countries.[55]

It is not denied that the national measures of control and expropriation may have the effect of impeding foreign investment and, in that way, contributing to the economic handicaps of the poorer states. In many cases, on the other hand, the hard reality of the need for capital and technology brings about agreements based on quid pro quos satisfactory to both sides and giving the foreign investor at least a short-range assurance of an adequate return on and recovery of his investments. Consequently, the actual significance of the concept of permanent sovereignty in reducing economic inequality can be determined only in the context of particular cases and the rather complicated circumstances of each national economy. But it is plain enough that the emphasis placed on that concept by almost the entire community of have-not states reveals their concern over the economic penetration by the transnational companies.[56] Such economic penetration is considered in many cases to be a threat to internal measures of social justice, income distribution, or the greater participation of disadvantaged groups in the national political process.[57] It should also be noted that several of the industrialized countries have placed importance on their sovereignty over resources in order to reject what they regard as excessive economic penetration by multinational companies.[58]

While these concerns reflect the interdependence of the contemporary economic world, they do not reveal a diminution in the demand for national autonomy. On the contrary, the objective reality of interdependence has clearly intensified the subjective feelings against excessive dependence on others. It would therefore be a mistake to consider the idea of permanent sovereignty over resources as anachronistic nationalistic rhetoric. It should be viewed as a fresh manifestation of present aspirations for self-rule and greater equality. One cannot forget, in the words of a perceptive United Nations official that "the historical circumstances of decolonization, memories of exploitation and the persistence of unequal bargaining powers have created the atmosphere in which foreign investment is now being judged." [59] At the same time, as he notes, the principle of sovereignty over resources needs to be reconciled with the "inescapable fact that non-renewable resources acquire value largely through international markets and they can be exploited only through the most complex technological and logistic operations." [60] Moreover, it is undeniable that most of the developing countries require foreign capital and foreign entrepreneurship to utilize their labor force and improve their standard of living. These facts underlie the ambivalence in the attitudes and legislation of many of the developing countries: on the one hand their desire for unhampered control and, on the other, the incentives they offer to attract foreign capital. This apparent contradiction cannot be dismissed as irrational; it should be understood as reflecting a polarity inherent in the objective circumstances and, in that sense, as a challenge to seek a reconciliation that would, to the extent possible, maximize the competing values.

In considering specific measures toward that end, it is important to take into account the changing relationship of host country and foreign investor in a typical resource development project. In the first stage, the government of the host country, anxious to exploit its natural resources, is conscious of its lack of capital, knowledge, and skilled personnel. It has to induce an investor to make a substantial outlay under conditions of considerable uncertainty, with a return to him not possible until large sums of money have been sunk into the operation and a high degree of production achieved. The risk is increased by the fact that fixed costs are relatively high, and there is little opportunity to adjust output in operations. In such circumstances, the bargaining power is heavily weighted on the side of the foreign investor, and generally inducements are offered by host countries to attract him. But the psychological relationship changes when the investment proves successful and the uncertainty and risk disappear. At that point the original terms of the concession seem excessively favorable to the investor, and the host government views its long-range commitment as a mistake.[61] As experience in Latin America and the Middle East indicates, the government then feels impelled to increase its share of taxes or royalties or to nationalize the company or compel transfer of ownership to local nationals.[62] The issue of "sanctity of contract" versus national sovereignty comes to the forefront and produces tension and a sense of injustice in both parties.

The justifications advanced by the developing countries for terminating or renegotiating contracts usually take a more specific form than a general claim of "changed circumstances" or sovereignty. They may, for example, charge duress or fraud in obtaining the concession. Disclosures of bribery and coercion by multinational corporations in many developing countries indicate that there may often be good reasons for governments to repudiate earlier commitments.[63] Foreign investors are probably increasingly aware that they risk such repudiation when they engage in illegal practices or in the kind of hard bargaining that may involve coercive or fraudulent aspects. Apart from calling for higher standards of conduct, remedies may be provided through improvements in national regulatory measures or possibly through international measures for greater accountability. I shall return to this later.

Another justification often put forward by the governments of developing countries is that the companies have received windfall profits. Sometimes this is linked to the claim that more favorable terms were given to other countries in similar agreements and that such discriminatory treatment is inequitable. Even within developed national societies the problem of determining excess profits is obviously a complicated one, and it becomes especially contentious in the relatively high-risk investment setting of the developing countries. Nevertheless, renegotiation may be justifiable on the ground that excessive or windfall profits have been obtained in the carrying out of a government contract. This is widely accepted by the industrialized countries: witness, the renegotiation procedures under United States law (which have even been applied to cases of alleged excess profits on overseas investment).[64] There is no reason why renegotiation on a similar basis should not be accepted in contractual arrangements between foreign companies and developing governments, provided that adequate procedures are available for a fair determination. It should be borne in mind that the problem of determining whether profits are excessive is especially difficult for developing countries dealing with large foreign companies.[65] We have already observed (in our discussion of the transfer of technology) the difficulties involved in so-called transfer pricing in situations where a multinational corporation can manipulate the prices it charges a local subsidiary and the costs it allocates to the subsidiary.[66] In this way, a foreign company can limit its taxable profits (or increase them in a "tax haven"). Since the local government cannot investigate the books of the home company, it is limited to seeking evidence of arms-length transaction prices of a similar kind, an inquiry which is generally difficult to pursue. In some cases, a developing country simply prorates the consolidated profits of a multinational company on the basis of an assessment of the contribution made by the local operation in that country. More commonly, a normal or "reasonable" return is fixed and attributed to the foreign company for purposes of taxation. The issue tends to become more difficult when a government that has nationalized or divested a foreign company claims that excessive profits have been made in past years and should now be set off against claims for compensation. These cases are not brought before international bodies and are generally left to negotiation with the parties or, in some cases, on the diplomatic level with the government of the home country. We do not have international criteria of excess profits, and the cases that arise are often influenced by political and ideological factors. It should be noted that in their home countries multinational companies are often compensated for losses by tax credits or investment risk insurance. Nonetheless, the issue of unjust enrichment and windfall profits remains a thorny problem and a frequent basis for demanding new contractual terms or new taxation.

One of the remedies proposed to meet the demands for the renegotiation of concessions is a divestment (or fade-out) provision.[67] It is contended that a policy of anticipated divestment built into the contracts with foreign companies would avoid the impasse that occurs when a government feels impelled to make radical changes in an existing agreement. Such fade-out provisions might well be acceptable to the company if provisions for compensation are agreed to in advance and if assurance is given that such compensation would be paid (perhaps by creating an escrow fund held by an independent party). The investor might then feel sufficiently protected to undertake the venture on a relatively short-term basis. It should be noted that divestment would not necessarily help the host country in a financial sense or in its development program, since the divestment might induce investors to lay stress on quick returns and to reduce their input of technology. Moreover, the host country might have to provide new capital at high cost and assume the risks of failure. But, as against these disadvantages to the host country, there would generally be a gain in avoiding situations of sudden termination and confrontation which would lead to protests of confiscation and could reduce the flow of foreign capital and technology.

From the standpoint of the foreign company there may be an advantage not only in receiving compensation but also in having the opportunity to make new arrangements under which the company would provide technical services or obtain long-term contracts to purchase materials from the venture which it formerly owned. It is interesting to note that several of the developed countries (for example, the United Kingdom, West Germany, and Denmark) have utilized their government development companies to finance the transfer of foreign enterprises to local ownership.[68] The International Finance Corporation, an affiliate of the International Bank for Reconstruction and Development, has also financed such transfers. The Andean (Cartagena) Treaty has laid down a policy which requires foreign private enterprises to divest themselves gradually of ownership in favor of local interests. The acceptability of this policy to the industrialized countries is also indicated by the fact that a group of leading companies and banks in developed countries established ADELA, an investment company for Latin American joint ventures, which has, as one of its primary aims, divestment in due course. There are clearly advantages to both the multinational companies and to the host countries in such planned fade-out arrangements under which the companies receive a reasonable return on their equity (and appropriate tax advantages) and local interests take over the enterprise with technical services continued (if needed) under contractual arrangements with the divested company. Though this course appears to be mutually advantageous, it runs into obstacles when governments seek to recover the high profits made in the past or when the companies resist divestment (sometimes through pressures of their home governments). In appropriate cases international financial institutions—both public and private—could take steps to reduce the obstacles by providing expert advice and some degree of financial support to facilitate the divestment process.

Arrangements under which foreign assistance is provided through service contracts or management contracts do not invite the criticism directed at equity ownership,[69] even though such arrangements may not necessarily be more economic for the host country. Still other techniques are useful in raising capital for natural resource development without direct ownership: for example, financial institutions have raised funds for developing countries through various types of factoring by selling collection rights to long-term contracts. In other cases, processors or customers have advanced money for contracts in return for an assured supply during an agreed period of operation. In all these cases, the tensions that arise from foreign control are eliminated or reduced significantly.

As I have already noted, the ability of host countries to deal on an equal basis with large foreign enterprises and protect their own interest is also a function of knowledge and skill, particularly when handling highly technical engineering, accounting, and legal matters. Recent United Nations reports have placed considerable stress on the potential role of international institutions in providing information to host countries that will strengthen their position in dealing with multinational corporations.[70] This would call not only for data and analysis but also for training experts in negotiation and administration and providing technical advisory teams to the governments of the developing countries. Beyond such fairly obvious assistance (which is not as easy to carry out as it may seem), proposals have been made for international procedures involving the disclosure and evaluation of multinational company practices and agreements.

These proposals, like those involving technical advice, would require a high level of technical expertise in the international organizations concerned; they would also call for the maintenance of exemplary standards of integrity and impartiality in order to safeguard the confidentiality and fairness of the information-gathering system.[71] Understandably questions may arise as to whether these conditions can be met in an international organization that is intensely political in its legislative organs and bureaucratic in its administration. One must conclude that in this, as in the other matters we have discussed, the objective of international social justice demands not only the development of new obligations and of new procedures, but also of an expanded international public service composed of persons of talent, vigor, and dedication. Despite frustrations, that does not seem an unrealistic goal.[72]

There have been several proposals for more comprehensive international regulation of multinational corporations, even though the proponents recognize that this would not be attainable in the immediate future. The idea of a code of conduct for multinational companies embodied in a treaty has been put forward in the United Nations by both the developing and the developed countries.[73] It is pointed out that many multinational corporations operate without

fully effective public control over their financial and managerial affairs, and that a treaty would fill an important gap in
the international legal system. This would be especially
helpful to the developing countries which often find it difficult to impose national controls and are handicapped in
negotiating with companies who can obtain more favorable
terms elsewhere. It is also contended that the multinational
corporations would gain if there were ground rules and a
mechanism to regulate the relations between the company
and the host government. George Ball, a leading advocate
of this position, has proposed a treaty that would establish
an international companies law, administered by representatives drawn from signatory countries, with rules, similar to
those in treaties of establishment, to govern the conduct of
host governments and the foreign corporations.[74] An international company which met certain conditions (for example, operation in a number of countries, multinational
management, etc.) would be qualified to apply for a charter,
under which it would receive the protection accorded by the
treaty in return for surveillance and compliance with the
basic rules. Ball has suggested that a treaty of this kind
should be instituted by the major trading countries, with the
objective of obtaining wider adherence over the years by the
developing countries.[75] An alternative course, suggested in
the United Nations, would be to formulate a comprehensive
nonbinding set of guidelines or code of conduct to function
as standards with the aim, in due course, of incorporation
into a multinational agreement.[76] No informed observer
believes that an effective code of conduct will be easily
achieved. Some observers think that an effort in that direction would be futile and perhaps counterproductive, especially if sought on a global basis.[77] Others are hopeful that
the attempt to spell out criteria and rules of permissible and
impermissible conduct would contribute to a more rational

and comprehensive understanding of the issues and would, in time, result in a code that would be advantageous to both governments and companies. Admittedly this would not do away with the underlying conflicts of interest but, as in the case of other structures of authority, it could provide a framework for the resolution of conflicts and reduce the friction and misunderstanding that now seems widespread. For this reason, the proposal for some form of international companies law will probably remain high on the agenda of international organizations and, with an improved political climate, it could eventually achieve general acceptance.

World Food Security

To discuss the equitable sharing of food in today's world cannot but involve an emotional and poignant element. "No tragedy," the secretary of state recently said "is more wounding than the look of despair in the eyes of a starving child." [78] The apparent inability to prevent starvation in one country, though ample food is available elsewhere, remains one of the most dispiriting facts of our present international order. How is it that the age-old gulf between the starving and the well-fed still persists despite miracle grains and advanced agricultural technology? And why is the response to famine in poor countries almost always too little and too late? There is no shortage of explanations. It is not difficult to trace the causes of scarcities and maldistribution to the misguided agricultural policies of governments in both the rich and the poor countries. Many have done so. Pricing controls, subsidies, discrimination against small farmers, misplaced restrictions on production and marketing, neglect of transport and storage, protectionism in developed countries, are the factors often indicated—and the list can

be extended.[79] Added to the defects of governmental policy, and not entirely divorced from them, are the natural
calamities—the creeping "desertification," the increase in
soil erosion, the shortage of water, the depredations of in-
sect and vermin especially in storage and transport, and the
dramatic changes in precipitation and temperature in several regions.[80] These natural factors may often be related to
the spread of industry and the movements of people, but
they are not easily subject to social controls. The diagnosis
of the crisis in food must also take account of the vast increase in the demand for food, largely attributable to the
general growth of population and to the marked trend, particularly in the developed countries, toward greater food
consumption of animal protein as against the much more
economical direct consumption of grains.[81] It is obvious that
the demand aspect of the food problem requires remedial
action along with the many-sided efforts needed to increase
the available food supply.

The effect of food shortages is most striking and tragic
in the so-called Fourth World—the poorest and neediest
countries. These include particularly countries such as those
on the Indian subcontinent where population pressures are
severe and those African countries which lack arable land
or the technology to utilize the resources which they have.
It is perhaps necessary to remind ourselves that not only in
these countries but in many other better-endowed lands,
malnutrition and hunger are the fate, not of the country in
its entirety, but of its poor and disadvantaged sectors: the
peasants with least buying power, the landless in the country, and the unemployed in the city.[82] In actuality "food security" in most countries of the world is closely linked to the
inequitable distribution of income.

It would, however, be a mistake to treat the food problem as one of direct concern only to the severely disadvan-

taged groups. The scarcities and instability of the world
food supply have profound effects on the economies of all
countries. The striking increases in food prices, linked to
world shortages, have had a significant role in stimulating
the rampant inflation in the developed countries. Fluctuat-
ing prices have disrupted industries dependent on food and
have brought new controls on exports of foodstuffs and agricultural supplies which have worsened the world situation.
As a result tendencies toward the liberalization of international trade have been reversed, and protectionism and au-
tarchical moves have been stimulated. Beyond these direct
consequences, there are the more profound effects of instability, inflation, widespread malnutrition, and the sense of
increased vulnerability throughout the world. It cannot be
doubted that the problem of world food security must be
seen not simply as a matter of charity or of improved trade
and functioning markets. It clearly requires profound
changes in national policy, in social habits, and in the development of international structures based on the premise of
a common responsibility for global needs.

A first significant step in this direction has been taken
in the recent World Food Conference and in a series of
related intergovernmental actions. The principle of a common responsibility has been articulated and applied as a
basis for a set of subsidiary norms and multinational mechanisms designed to reduce the risk of starvation and malnutrition in various parts of the world.

One of the central features of the World Food Conference plan is an undertaking by the countries of the world to
build up and maintain national stocks of cereals, including
reserves, on the basis of internationally determined requirements.[83] In combination these stocks would provide a minimum level of basic food stocks for the world as a whole.
The Food and Agriculture Organization would assess world

needs and supplies, and it would lay down guidelines for the reserves to be maintained by all countries, not only for their own domestic needs but also for export to others in case of crop failure or national disaster. These actions would be supported by procedures for consultation on the adequacy of national stocks of grain and the action required to meet any difficulty. To give these collective efforts an adequate factual foundation, the countries would undertake to furnish information on crop conditions, stock levels, and prospective exports and imports. In addition, a whole series of international measures would be taken to assist countries, especially in the developing world. This series would include, particularly, expansion of fertilizer production, improvement of water supply, assistance in creating food reserves, and technical assistance in all phases of agriculture.

Critics will be quick to observe that this embryonic security scheme rests on the fragile foundation of voluntary cooperation among diverse governments. Its defenders will point to the shortcomings of the rival approaches. On the one side, a free market approach—exceedingly valuable in producing more efficient allocation of resources—is clearly not adequate to provide the requisite security of a reserve to meet natural disasters (now almost endemic) or the chronic deficits of the most deprived countries. On the other side, the establishment of a world food bank or international "ever-normal" granary requires the acceptance of centralized international decision making in respect to matters regarded as vital to domestic well-being. It would be unrealistic to expect the major exporting countries, in particular the United States, to entrust an international agency with the management and control of the substantial stockpiles of food stocks required for a level of safety in present conditions. However, the new scheme, while acknowledging the desirability of national discretion in many respects, sets up a

structure for international coordination that goes beyond a
purely voluntary system of assistance. It can be seen that to
achieve an effective security system, a series of agreements
and rules will be required [84]—in particular, the following:

—agreement by the participants on the size of the reserve required for security;

—agreement on an equitable allocation of reserve hold-
ings by the individual countries (taking into account their
productive capacity, domestic requirements, and trade);

—rules for the building up of reserves in times of good
harvest;

—guidelines for the storage and maintenance of reserves by the national governments;

—rules for releasing supplies in the stockpiles in response to needs (possibly on the basis of objective indica-
tors);

—possibly priority rules for recipients, as for example,
special rights to the neediest countries;

—rules for the timely furnishing of data on agricultural
production, export availabilities, import requirements, existing stocks, and other relevant items.

This list indicates that even within a system of voluntary cooperation, it will be necessary to have a fairly elaborate framework of rules and agreements adopted by the
governments on matters of considerable practical importance. It would not be farfetched to see in this a body of
"world food law" that might in time develop beyond the
minimal requirements of food security.

Valuable as a system of worldwide reserves may be, it is
essential to go beyond that if food security is to be attained.
The highest priority, all agree, is for a well-sustained effort
to increase production in the developing countries. While

this is principally the responsibility of national governments, the role of the international community is now seen as significant and perhaps crucial. It is believed that only through international stimulation will most of the countries take the steps required to improve—and, in most cases, restructure—their agriculture. This can no longer be thought of as a matter of technical assistance or the sending of seeds and fertilizers. It is recognized as a deep-seated political and social problem which will involve alterations in power and privilege. The ability of international agencies to effect such profound changes depends, in large part, on their propagation of ideas that are well-founded in experience and implemented in practice. Recent events have indicated how the lessons of national experience have been given wider significance as they have become the ideas of international experts, and how these ideas have gathered strength when linked into a coherent pattern for action. The action itself is stimulated by the collaboration between the international experts and the national officialdom—both parts of a fairly well-knit transnational professional network. Such action can also be more effectively promoted by international agencies when, as in the case of the World Bank, they have a clear strategy of reform and the funds to carry out projects within national societies.

As one example of that strategy, I draw attention to the priority accorded to the small individual farmer under the program of the World Bank.[85] This strategy rests on the evidence gathered from diverse agricultural systems indicating that labor-intensive, small farming within a cooperative framework can do most to increase production in the developing world. The World Bank sees this (to quote Barbara Ward) as a "hard-headed calculation that small farmers, working for goals and returns they understand, on land where they have security of tenure and with enough coop-

erative credit and services to enrich their labor, produce the
world's highest returns per worker and often per acre." [86]
Miss Ward goes on to say that "it is upon this strategy of
backing the small men—the half-billion small farmers in the
developing world—that the hopes of feeding most of mankind in the longer term depend." There is within this strategy a conception of social policy that would involve far-
reaching changes in the structure of agriculture and in the
political communities concerned. The fact that it has been
adopted as the official policy of the World Bank and backed
by its resources (as well as by the World Food Conference) [87] cannot be regarded as merely a technical or administrative fact. It should be regarded as an indication of
international public policy—still perhaps in embryo—which
may, in time, give rise to firm expectations about the proper
behavior of governments and international bodies in this
vital area. One must recognize that this will only come about
if in actual fact the strategy of the World Bank and the
other agencies concerned is carried out. For that verdict, we
need to wait. However, from the standpoint of our theme,
the example is important in demonstrating that a far-
reaching normative principle may emanate from the decision of international operational agencies and be given
practical effect through activities within the domestic jurisdiction of the states concerned. That this principle of aiding
the small land-holding farmer has a significant bearing on
the goal of equitable sharing is clear enough. It will affect
not only the availability of food to those in need but also
improve the relative status and dignity of a large segment of
disadvantaged mankind.

It is not inconceivable that the food crisis may give rise
to a new international normative conception relative to the
consumption of food. I have already mentioned the relevance of dietary patterns to the problem of scarcity. There

is an increasing body of evidence that consumption on the upper level of the food chain carries with it a double penalty. In the first and most obvious way, it constitutes a heavy drain on basic foodstuffs and an excessively high per capita claim on agricultural resources which are needed to meet malnutrition and famine in deficit areas.[88] Secondly, persuasive evidence indicates that a diet high in animal and dairy foods is in itself a form of malnutrition in view of its contribution to cardiovascular diseases and other degenerative conditions.[89] Though both of these consequences are still regarded as primarily within the domestic concerns of governments, their clear international implications have brought the issue of consumption patterns to the international agenda. One country, Norway, presented evidence to the World Food Conference on its experience in carrying out national nutrition programs which involved a substantial reduction in the fattier grain-fed meats and an increase in consumption of grains and vegetables. That program, it was indicated, had reduced the grain imports required, cut down on the land, water, energy, and fertilizer needed in Norway, and improved the health and life expectancy of its inhabitants.[90] If the conclusions reached in Norway are substantiated by further experience there and elsewhere, there would be good reason to expect the issue to become a matter of international concern and a subject of international recommendation to national states. Should the food shortages continue and mass starvation occur, it is not inconceivable that the recommendatory principle will move into the realm of the prescriptive. As I observed earlier, when there is a common perception of right and duty on the part of the states concerned, and when that perception is expressed as a norm in international bodies and acted upon by the states, we have, for all intents and purposes, a rule of law. One hopes that the crisis will not arise, but if it should,

one would also hope that there will be a common perception of right and duty on the part of the well-fed, substantiated by their behavior. If not, C. P. Snow's somber proph-
ecy made some years ago will be borne out—that
megadeaths in starving lands, watched on affluent peoples'
television screens, could mark the end of any moral community for man.[91]

Conclusion

The dramatic image evoked by Lord Snow reminds us that
the sharing of the world's resources involves more than considerations of economic gain and bargaining. It is bound
up, in a profound sense, with ideas of morality and justice
that are part of the fundamental conceptions of the way in
which the affairs of society should be conducted. These
conceptions differ, of course. The differences reflect varia-
tions in historical development, material factors, social
ideals, and perceived opportunities. It is not surprising that
in specific cases they produce disagreement as to what is fair
and just.

Yet, as we have seen, there is a widespread tendency in
international decisions to apply standards of equity to the
allocation of resources. That tendency is not derived solely
or mainly from moral idealism; it has its origin and basis
principally in the necessities of contemporary international
relations. For it is a salient fact of international life today
that the national states faced with imbalances and deficits
and with intensified competition for a larger share of the
world's wealth are compelled to enter into cooperative arrangements and devise means of resolving competing demands. To achieve this in particular situations, they must
have a basic agreement or shared conception of principle

for the distribution of benefits and burdens. Without such agreement, it becomes virtually impossible for governments with divergent interests to maintain continuing cooperation and a stable association.[92] It is this requirement that provides the basis for the application of standards of equity in international decisions. The ideal of distributive justice may thus be seen as grounded in the rocky soil of international conflict and the felt necessities of collaboration.

How that broad and vague ideal can be given determinate content and political force has been a principal focus of this book. We have observed that normative and juridical criteria have evolved and been applied in various contexts—for example, to oil, fish, minerals, food, water, air, technology, foreign investment, and trade. We have also seen that principles of entitlement have been related to need, acquired rights, notions of equality, self-rule, the concept of a common heritage, the rectification of past injustices, the demands for economic development, and the growing concern over environmental threats. Our analysis has indicated how international mechanisms and procedures have been created and used in determining entitlements and in resolving competing demands. The role of law has been considered in instrumental terms as a process for attaining distributive justice and other social ends and for facilitating rationality in decisions.

It might perhaps be charged that I have been too optimistic. One might question the emphasis placed on the common interest in international cooperation and in achieving just solutions. We are, after all, still in a world marked by profound conflicts of interest and strong nationalist sentiment. Nor can we be at all confident that collective decisions on the allocation of resources will better serve our major objectives than a decentralized system governed by market forces. Clearly, there are substantial political limitations on the capacity of the international community to meet the demands for equitable sharing and higher standards of living. For these and for other reasons it would be foolish to conclude that we are at long last likely to achieve distributive justice among nations. Yet it would be almost as foolish to underestimate the trends we have described. The normative principles and the cooperative arrangements which have emerged are grounded, as we have seen, in the necessities of a common predicament. It would not be realistic to expect that they will fade away or that the deeply rooted human demand for a fair and just order will disappear.

Notes

Part I
International Equity
and Its Dilemmas

1. I have borrowed this phrase from Professor Julius Stone, though he has used it to apply to communities rather than to international organs. See Julius Stone, *Social Dimensions of Law and Justice* (Stanford: Stanford University Press, 1966), pp. 117, 796–98.

2. Oscar Schachter, "Toward a Theory of International Obligation," in *The Effectiveness of International Decisions*, ed. Stephen Schwebel (Leyden: Sijthoff; Dobbs Ferry, N.Y.: Oceana, 1971), pp. 9–31. See also Rosalyn Higgins, *The Development of International Law Through the Political Organs of the United Nations* (London, New York: Oxford University Press, 1963); Jorge Castañeda, *Legal Effects of United Nations Resolutions* (New York: Columbia University Press, 1969); A. J. P. Tammes, "Decisions of International Organs as Sources of Law," in *94 Hague Academy Recueil des Cours 1958* (Leyden: Sijthoff, 1959), 2: 264–364.

3. Karl Marx, *Critique of the Gotha Programme* (New York: International Publishers, 1938), p. 10.

4. See International Commission on Development (Pearson Commission), *Partners in Development* (New York: Praeger, 1969), chapter 7 and tables 15–19; Robert Asher, *Development Assistance in the Seventies* (Washington: Brookings Institution, 1970), pp. 19–38. For discussions of the legal implications, see Michel Virally, "La 2ème Décennie des Nations Unies pour le développement—Essai d'interprétation para-juridique," in *Ann. Française de droit int.* (Paris: Centre National de la Recherche Scientifique, 1970), 16: 28–33.

5. Pope Paul VI, *Populorum Progressio,* Papal Encyclical of 26 March 1967, paragraphs 23, 49. See also "Charter on the Economic Rights and Duties of States," U.N. General Assembly resolution 3281 (XXIX), 12 Dec. 1974.

6. Gunnar Myrdal, "The World Poverty Problem" in *Britannica Book of the Year, 1971,* p. 34. On unequal income distribution in less-developed countries, see Irma Adelman and Cynthia Taft Morris, *Economic Growth and Social Equity in Developing Countries* (Stanford: Stanford University Press, 1973), a comprehensive and cogent analysis of the failure of "trickle down" in developing countries and of the concentration of benefits at the upper end of the income spectrum.

7. References to these views are found in John Rawls, *A Theory of Justice* (Cambridge: Harvard University Press, 1971), pp. 290–91.

8. Mihajlo Mesarovic and Eduard Pestel, *Mankind at the Turning Point* (New York: E. P. Dutton, 1974); see also Jan Tinbergen, "Assigning World Priorities," in *Environment and Society in Transition,* ed. P. Albertson and M. Barnett (New York: New York Academy of Sciences, 1975), pp. 25–31.

9. Ernst B. Haas, "On Systems and International Regimes," *World Politics* 27, no. 2 (January 1975): 147–74.

10. Philippe de Seynes, "Prospects for a Future Whole World," *International Organization* 26 (Winter 1972): 1–17.

11. Raul Prebisch and César Furtado in Latin America and Samir Amin in Africa have expressed this view. See Samir Amin, *Accumulation on a World Scale* (New

York: Monthly Review Press, 1974); Norman Girvan, "Economic Nationalism," *Daedalus* 104 (Fall 1975): 146–50. A comprehensive historical study based on a similar conception is to be found in Immanuel Wallerstein, *The Modern World-System: Capitalist Agriculture and the Origins of the European World Economy* (New York: Academic Press, 1974).

12. Aristotle *Nicomachean Ethics,* Book V, 3.

13. See International Court of Justice, *Reports,* (1974), p. 3, Judgment, Fisheries Jurisdiction (United Kingdom v. Iceland); Judge Dillard's separate opinion notes the relevance of the Aristotelean conception of distributive justice, ibid., p. 71. See also International Court of Justice, *Reports* (1969), Judgment, North Sea Continental Shelf Cases, especially the separate opinion of Judge Jessup, pp. 67–84.

14. More detailed reference to these situations will be found in Parts II and III.

15. A similar conclusion on the rectification of past injustice was reached by Robert Nozick in his *Anarchy, State and Utopia* (New York: Basic Books, 1975), which, from a conservative perspective, places emphasis on the legitimacy and justice of entitlements derived from the historical process that led to them.

16. U.N. General Assembly, "Declaration on the Establishment of a New International Economic Order," paragraph 4f of U.N. General Assembly resolution 3201 (S-VI), 1 May 1974.

17. Edmund S. Phelps, ed., *Economic Justice* (Middlesex, England: Penguin Books, Ltd., 1973), p. 22.

18. Kenneth Arrow, "Values and Collective Decision-Making" in Phelps, ed., *supra* n. 17, pp. 117–36.

19. See, for example, the proposals of Secretary of State Henry Kissinger to the U.N. General Assembly, 7th Special Session, U.N. Doc. A/PV.2327, 1 Sept. 1975, pp. 16–65. See also Richard Gardner, "The Hard Road to World Order," *Foreign Affairs* 52 (1974): 566; Thomas O. Enders, "OPEC and the Industrial Countries," *Foreign Affairs* 53 (1975): 625; U.N. Report of Experts, "A New United Nations Structure for Global Economic Co-operation," U.N. Doc. E/AC.62/9, 28 May 1975, pp. 30–32.

20. See U.N. General Assembly resolution 3129 (XXVIII), 13 Dec. 1973, and report of Executive Director of U.N. Environmental Programme on "Cooperation in the Field of the Environment Concerning Natural Resources Shared by Two or More States," U.N. Doc. UNEP/GC/44, 20 Feb. 1975, pp. 41–45.

21. Economic coercion directed against the sovereign rights and independence of any state has been declared to be in violation of international law by several declarations of the U.N. General Assembly. See article 32 of the "Charter of Economic Rights and Duties of States" (U.N. Gen. Ass. res. 3281 [XXIX]), the "Declaration of Principles of International Law concerning Friendly Relations of States" (U.N. Gen. Ass. res. 2625 [XXV], 24 Oct. 1970) and the "Declaration on the Inadmissibility of Intervention" (U.N. Gen. Ass. res. 2131 [XX], 20 Dec. 1965). For discus-

sions of the legality of economic coercion see D. W. Bowett, "Economic Coercion and Reprisal by States," *Virginia J. Int. Law* 13 (1972): 1; Gardner, *supra* n.19; R. B. Lillich, "Economic Coercion and the International Legal Order," *Int. Affairs* (London) 51 (1975): 358; J. J. Paust and A. P. Blaustein, "The Arab Oil Weapon—a Threat to International Peace," *Am. J. Int. Law* 68 (1974): 410; I. Shihata, "Destination Embargo of Arab Oil: Its Legality under International Law," *Am. J. Int. Law* 68 (1974): 591.

22. See discussions in U.N. General Assembly, 29th session, plenary meetings, December 1974, U.N.Docs. A/PV.2307, A/PV.2308, A/PV.2313, A/PV.2314, A/PV.2316.

23. See papers and proceedings in Schwebel, ed., *supra* n.2.

24. For a general review of diverse voting procedures see Inis Claude, *Swords into Ploughshares*, 4th ed. (New York: Random House, 1971), pp. 118–62. Specific procedures are discussed in F. Y. Chai, *Consultation and Consensus in the Security Council* (New York: UNITAR, 1971); Elizabeth McIntyre, "Weighted Voting in International Organization," *Int. Org.* 8 (1954): 484–97; Oscar Schachter, "Conciliation Procedures in the United Nations Conference on Trade and Development," *Liber Amicorum for Martin Domke* (The Hague: Nijhoff, 1967), pp. 268–74; Louis Sohn, "Voting Procedures in United Nations Conferences for the Codification of International Law," *Am. J. Int. Law* 69 (1975): 310–53.

25. Edward S. Mason and Robert E. Asher, *The World Bank since Bretton Woods* (Washington, D.C.: Brookings Institution, 1973); Robert Jackson, *A Study of the Capacity of the UN Development System*, 2 vols. (New York: United Nations, 1969).

Part II
Sharing the
Common Heritage

1. See John G. Ruggie, "Collective Goods and Future International Collaboration," *Am. Pol. Sci. Rev.* 66 (September 1972): 874–93. The concept of public goods was developed principally by economists in the field of public finance. See John G. Head, "Public Goods and Public Policy," *Public Finance* 17 (1962): 197–219; Richard Musgrave, *The Theory of Public Finance* (New York: McGraw-Hill, 1959). Public goods in relation to organizations is dealt with in Mancur Olson, Jr., *The Logic of Collective Action*, rev. ed. (New York: Schocken, 1971), pp. 14–16.

2. See U.N. Secretary-General, "Economic Implications of Sea-Bed Mineral Development in the International Area," U.N. Doc. A/CONF.62/25, 22 May 1974; U.N. Secretary-General, "Marine Questions—Uses of the Sea," U.N. Doc. E/5650, 30 Apr. 1975.

3. See Louis Henkin, *Law for the Sea's Mineral Resources*, Columbia University Institute for the Study of Science in Human Affairs Monograph No. 1, 1968; M. S. McDougal and W. Burke, *The Public Order of the Oceans* (New Haven: Yale University

Press, 1962); C. A. Colliard, R. J. Dupuy, et al., *Le Fond des Mers* (Paris: Armand Colin, 1971).

4. Giulio Pontecorvo, ed., *Fisheries Conflicts in the North Atlantic: Problems of Management and Jurisdiction* (Cambridge, Mass.: Ballinger, 1974), p. xviii. For a discussion of the economics of fishing, see F. T. Christy, Jr. and Anthony Scott, *The Common Wealth in Ocean Fisheries* (Baltimore: Johns Hopkins Press, 1965).

5. International Court of Justice, *Reports* (1951), p. 116, Judgment, Fisheries Case (United Kingdom v. Norway).

6. International Court of Justice, *Reports* (1974), p. 3, Judgment, Fisheries Jurisdiction (United Kingdom v. Iceland).

7. Ibid., pp. 24–26.

8. Ann Hollick, "What to Expect from a Sea Treaty," *Foreign Policy* 18 (1975): 76,777; John T. Swing, "Who Will Own the Oceans," *Foreign Affairs* 54 (1976): 533.

9. For the position of the landlocked states, see Thomas M. Franck, M. El Baradei, and G. Aron, "The New Poor: Landlocked, Shelflocked and other Geographically Disadvantaged States," *NYU Law Review* 7 (Spring 1974): 33–57; V. Ibler, "The Land and Shelflocked States and the Development of the Law of the Sea," *Annals of Int. Studies* (Geneva) 4 (1973): 55–65. For a comprehensive criticism of the economic zones, see Arvid Pardo and Elizabeth Borgese, *The New International Economic Order and the Law of the Sea* (Malta: International Ocean Institute, 1976).

10. See "Informal Single Negotiating Text" of Third Conference on Law of the Sea, U.N. Doc. A/CONF.62/WP.8/Parts 1, 2, and 3, May 1975. See also John R. Stevenson and Bernard H. Oxman, "The Third United Nations Conference on the Law of the Sea: the 1975 Geneva Session," *Amer. J. Int. Law* 69 (October 1975): 763–97. The New York session of the Law of the Sea Conference which ended in May 1976 confirmed the propositions set forth in the text.

11. See Henkin, *supra* n.3. See also Roy S. Lee, "Machinery for Seabed Mining: Some General Issues Before the Geneva Session of the Third United Nations Conference on the Law of the Sea," in *Law of the Sea: Caracas and Beyond*, Proceedings, Law of the Sea Institute 1975 (Cambridge, Mass.: Ballinger, 1975), pp. 117–66.

12. Giulio Pontecorvo, "Reflections on the Common Heritage of Mankind," *Ocean Development and Int. Law* 2 (1974): 203; J. L. Mero, "The Great Nodule Controversy," in *Law of the Sea: Caracas and Beyond, supra* n.11, pp. 117–660.

13. See "Informal Single Negotiating Text," *supra* n.10, Part 1, 7 May 1975.

14. Frank Njenga, representative of Kenya in remarks at Conference of the Law of the Sea Institute of the University of Rhode Island, Occasional Paper No. 24, December 1974, p. 21.

15. This proposal was advanced by Secretary of State Kissinger in an address in New York on April 8, 1976 on the Law of the Sea. See State Department Press Release No. 162. It did not win support from all developing countries.

16. These provisions were included in the 1975 "Informal Single Negotiating Text," Part 1 and remained substantially the same in the May 1976 version.

17. Francis T. Christy, Jr., *Alternative Arrangements for Marine Fisheries: An Overview* (Washington, D.C.: Resources for the Future: Program of Int. Studies of Fishery Arrangements, Paper No. 1, 1973), pp. 29–44.

18. American Society of International Law, *Principles for a Global Fisheries Management Régime,* in Studies on Transnational Legal Policy, no. 4 (Washington, D.C.: American Soc. Int. Law, 1974).

19. See Christy, *supra* n.17, chapter 3. Shigeru Oda, "Distribution of Fish Resources of the High Seas: Free Competition or Artificial Quotas," in *The Future of the Sea's Resources,* ed. L. M. Alexander (Kingston, R.I.: Law of the Sea Institute, 1968).

20. Douglas M. Johnston, *The International Law of Fisheries: A Framework for Policy-Oriented Inquiries* (New Haven: Yale University Press, 1965); F. T. Christy, Jr., "Fisheries Goals and the Rights of Property," *Transactions of the American Fisheries Society* 98 (April 1969): 369–78.

21. For a comprehensive treatment of law and practice, see A. H. Garretson, R. D. Hayton, and C. J. Olmstead, eds., *The Law of International Drainage Basins* (Dobbs Ferry, N.Y.: Oceana, 1967). See also F. J. Berber, *Rivers in International Law* (London: Stevens; New York: Oceana, 1959). Legislative texts and treaties on international rivers are found in U.N. Doc. Sales No. 63 V.4, 1963.

22. U.N. Secretary-General, "Report on International Water Resources Development," U.N. Doc. E/C.7/2/Add.6, January 1971.

23. See U.N. report, "Integrated River Basin Development," U.N. Sales No. E.70.II.A.4, 1970; C. B. Bourne, "The Development of International Water Resources: The Drainage Basin Approach," *Canadian Bar Review* 47 (1969): 62–87.

24. U.N. Report of Experts, "Management of International Water Resources: Institutional and Legal Aspects," U.N. Sales No. E.75.II.A.2, Doc. ST/ESA/5, 1975, paragraph 27.

25. Ibid., paragraph 38.

26. *Report of the Fifty-second Conference (1966) of the International Law Association held in Helsinki* (London: International Law Association, 1967), pp. 486 ff. Also reprinted as Annex 2 in U.N. Report, *supra* n.23.

27. See "Resolution of the Institute of International Law on the Utilization of Non-Maritime International Waters, Salzburg Session 1961," in *Ann. de l'Institut de droit int.* 49, tome 2 (1962): 381–84. For review of authorities, see W. W. Van Alstyne, "The Justiciability of International River Disputes," *Duke Law Journal* (1964): 307–40, esp. pp. 329–39, also works cited *supra.* n.21.

28. *U.S. Dept. State Bull.* 69 (1973): 338. See Herbert Brownell and S. D. Eaton, "The Colorado River Salinity Problem with Mexico," *Am. J. Int. Law* 69 (1975): 255; M. I. Bulson, "Colorado River Salinity Problem," *Int. Lawyer* 9 (1975): 283–94.

29. See also C. B. Bourne, "Procedure in the Development of International Drainage Basins," *Univ. of Toronto L. J.* 22 (1972): 172–91; idem in *Canadian Yearbook of Int. Law* 10 (1972): 212–34. The arbitral award in "Affaire de Lac Lanoux" has dicta supporting the obligation to notify and consult, *International Law Reports* 24 (1959): 101, 129–30, 138.

30. U.N. General Assembly resolution 3129 (XXVIII), 13 Dec. 1973. A similar provision is in the "Charter of Economic Rights and Duties of States," adopted by U.N. General Assembly resolution 3281 (XXIX), 12 Dec. 1974. Several states have denied that there is a general obligation requiring prior information and consultation. See, in particular, the views of Brazil in the debate on the above-mentioned resolution 3129 of the General Assembly, in U.N. Doc. A/C.2/SR.1564, 27 Nov. 1973, p. 20, and in its reply to an inquiry of the Executive Director of UNEP in U.N. Doc. UNEP/GC.44, 20 Feb. 1975, paragraph 9. Moreover, in this view, "shared resources" only applies where "sovereignty is shared" (e.g., contiguous rivers) but not to resources within one state (i.e., successive rivers).

31. For a discussion of these problems, see Bourne, *supra* n.29 and award in the Lac Lanoux Arbitration, *supra* n.29.

32. See Alexander Kiss and C. Lambrechts, "La lutte contre la pollution de l'eau en Europe Occidentale," *Ann. Français de droit int.* 15 (1969): pp. 728 ff.

33. Estimate by C. B. Bourne is based upon the index to the report of the Secretary-General on "Legal Problems relating to the Utilization of International Rivers," U.N. Doc. A/5409, 15 Apr. 1963. See also Garretson, Hayton and Olmstead, *supra* n.21.

34. L. M. Bloomfield and G. F. Fitzgerald, *Boundary Waters Problems of Canada and the United States* (Toronto: Carswell Co., 1958), pp. 39–40.

35. For a discussion of the Columbia River controversy, see Ralph W. Johnson, "The Columbia River," in Garretson, Hayton and Olmstead, eds., *supra* n.21, pp. 196–241. On the Great Lakes issues see R. B. Bilder, "Controlling Great Lakes Pollution," in *Law, Institutions and the Global Environment,* ed. L. Hargrove (Dobbs Ferry, N.Y.: Oceana, 1972), pp. 294–380.

36. See U.N. General Assembly resolution 3129 (XXVIII), 13 Dec. 1973, paragraph 3.

37. UNEP Executive Director, "Report on Cooperation in the Field of the Environment concerning Natural Resources shared by Two or More States," U.N. Doc. UNEP/GC/44, 20 Feb. 1975, pp. 41–45.

38. U.N. Reports of International Arbitral Awards, U.N.R.I.A.A., vol. 3, U.N. Sales No. 1949.V.2, pp. 1965–82; *Am. J. Int. Law* 35 (1941): 684–734.

39. See L. F. E. Goldie, "International Principles of Responsibility for Pollution," *Columbia J. Transnational Law* 9 (1970): 283; *Annuaire de l'Institut de droit international,* tome 2 (1969): 260–68; G. Handl, "Territorial Sovereignty and the Problem of Transnational Pollution, *Am. J. Intl. Law* 69 (1975): 50–76.

40. See National Academy of Sciences, *Weather and Climate Modification* (Washington, D.C.: Government Printing Office, 1973); C. F. Cooper and W. C. Jolly, *Ecological Effects of Weather Analysis* (Ann Arbor, Mich.: University of Michigan, 1969).

41. Harry Wexler, "Modifying Weather on a Large Scale," *Science* 128 (1968): 1059–63; P. M. Borisov, "Can We Control the Arctic Climate," *Bull, Atomic Scientists* 25 (1969): 43–48.

42. G. J. F. MacDonald, "How to Wreck the Environment," in *Unless Peace Comes*, ed. Nigel Calder (London: Penguin Press, 1968), p. 165. See also U.S. Congress, Senate, Committee on Foreign Relations, Subcommittee on Oceans and International Environment, *Prohibiting Military Weather Modification: Hearing on*, 92d Cong., 2d sess., 1973.

43. Massachusetts Institute of Technology, *S.M.I.C. Report on Inadvertent Weather Modification* (1971). See *UNESCO Courier* (September 1973) (special issue on weather modification).

44. R. A. Bryson, "A Perspective on Climatic Change," *Science* 184 (1974): 753–60; R. A. Bryson and W. M. Wendland, "Climatic Effects of Atmospheric Pollution," in *Global Effects of Environmental Pollution*, ed. S. F. Singer (New York: Springer Verlag, 1970), pp. 130–38.

45. H. J. and R. Taubenfeld, "Some International Implications of Weather Modification Activities," *Int. Org.* 23 (1969): 808–33. E. B. Weiss, "International Responses to Weather Modification," *Int. Org.* 29 (1975): 805; F. L. Kirgis, "Technological Challenge to the Shared Environment," *Am. J. Int. Law* 66 (1972): 290–320.

46. U.N. General Assembly resolution 3129 (XXVIII), 13 Dec. 1973.

47. See R. A. Howard, J. F. Matheson and D. W. North, "The Decision to Seed Hurricanes," *Science* 176 (1972): 1191–1203.

48. In addition to the U.N. Environmental Programme, the World Meteorological Organization (WMO) carries out monitoring and global research on weather and the atmosphere. See "World Meteorological Org., World Weather Watch: The Plan and Implementation Programme 1972–1975," WMO Doc., July 1972. Recommendation 70 of the Stockholm Conference on the Human Environment calls for prior consultation and information on activities that may have an appreciable risk of effects on climate. See also U.N. Doc. UNEP/GC/31, 1974, paragraphs 195–99.

49. The "Treaty on Outer Space" is found in U.N. General Assembly resolution 2222 (XXI), 19 Dec. 1966. See also J. F. S. Fawcett, *International Law and the Use of Outer Space* (Manchester, England: Manchester University Press, 1968), pp. 54, 60. The issue of injurious activities in outer space arose conspicuously as a result of the so-called "copper needles" experiment (Project West Ford) which threatened interference with other activities in space. See U.N. Doc. A/AC.105/15, 1963. For a comprehensive examination of resource problems in outer space, see M. S. Mc-

Dougal, H. D. Lasswell and Ivan Vlasic, *Law and Public Order in Space* (New Haven: Yale University Press, 1963).

50. See Wilfred Beckerman, *In Defence of Economic Growth* (London: Jonathan Cape, 1974), pp. 180–214, 241–48.

51. See Carl Christol, "The International Legal and Institutional Aspects of the Stratospheric Ozone Problem," a staff report prepared for the U.S. Senate Committee on Aeronautical and Space Sciences, 15 Aug. 1975, 94th Cong., 1st sess.

Part III
Equity in Distribution

1. See U.N. General Assembly resolution 3201 (S-VI), May 1974, paragraph 4j, and resolution 3202 (S-VI), May 1974, paragraph 1d. Numerous references to just-prices and equitable price relationships were made at the U.N. General Assembly, 6th Special Session on Raw Materials and Development in 1974. See, for example, statements of President Boumédienne of Algeria, U.N. Doc. A/PV.2208, pp. 31–32, 37; J. Amuzegar of Iran, A/PV.2209, pp. 103–10; M. Jobert of France, ibid., pp. 36–42; M. Perez-Guerrero of Venezuela, A/PV.2213, pp. 80 ff.; M. Stevens of Sierra-Leone, A/PV.2212, p. 6.

2. Statements of Secretary of State Henry Kissinger to the U.N. General Assembly, 6th Special Session, U.N. Doc. A/PV.2214, pp. 22–26; Foreign Minister Scheel, Federal Republic of Germany, A/PV.2209, pp. 56–57; D. Ennals, United Kingdom, A/PV.2209, p. 117. See also the statement of Secretary Kissinger to the U.N. General Assembly, 7th Special Session (delivered by Ambassador Moynihan), U.N. Doc. A/PV.2327, pp. 16–65, especially pp. 42–58.

3. Albertus Magnus and Thomas Aquinas were the leading proponents of this position. See Raymond de Roover, "Ancient and Medieval Economic Thought," *Int. Encyc. Social Sciences* 4 (1968): 433. For a detailed study see John W. Baldwin, *The Medieval Theories of the Just Price* (Philadelphia: American Philosophical Society, 1959).

4. See, for example, statements at the U.N. General Assembly, 6th Special Session, by representatives of Liberia, U.N. Doc. A/PV.2209, pp. 13–15; Sierra Leone, A/PV.2212, p. 6; Peru, A/PV.2213; Saudi Arabia, A/PV.2217, p. 31.

5. Chris Economides, "Should the Rich Countries Help the Poor?," in *The Gap Between Rich and Poor Nations*, Proceedings of a Conference held by the International Economic Association at Bled, Yugoslavia, 27 Aug.–2 Sept. 1970, ed. Gustav, Ranis (London: Macmillan, 1972), pp. 183–200.

6. For statements at the U.N. General Assembly, 6th Special Session, see Algeria, U.N. Doc. A/PV.2208, pp. 18–20; Iraq, A/PV.2217, p. 16; Zambia, A/PV.2211, pp. 101–02. See also note by UNCTAD secretary-general to Board of Trade and Development, August 1974, TD/B(XVI)/Misc. 3.

7. See Gottfried Haberler, *A Survey of International Trade Theory* (Princeton: Princeton University Press, 1961), chapter 4; Haberler, "Terms of Trade and Economic

Development," in *Economic Development for Latin America*, eds., H. S. Ellis and H. C. Wallich (London: Macmillan, 1961), pp. 275–97.

8. Many economists doubt that there has in fact been a downward trend in the terms on which primary products exchange with manufactures. For example, see M. K. Atallah, *The Long-Term Movement of the Terms of Trade Between Agricultural and Industrial Products* (Rotterdam: Netherlands Economics Institute, 1958).

9. U.N. Secretary-General, "Evolution of Basic Commodity Prices since 1950," U.N. Doc. A/9544, 2 Apr. 1974 and U.N. Doc. A/9544, Add.1, 4 Apr. 1974.

10. U.N. General Assembly resolution 3202 (S-VI) notes that the countries which are most seriously affected by high prices are the least developed, the landlocked, and those with low per capita income. A list of criteria of needs is set forth in Part 10 of the resolution.

11. See "Programme of Action for a New International Economic Order," U.N. General Assembly resolution 3202 (S-VI), Part 1 on raw materials and primary commodities.

12. See, for example, statements at the U.N. General Assembly, 6th Special Session, by representatives of Kenya, U.N. Doc. A/PV.2224, pp. 8–10 and Thailand, A/PV.2220, pp. 47–50.

13. See the statements cited *supra* n.6 by representatives of Algeria, Iraq, and Zambia.

14. For a sophisticated discussion of this issue, see Raymond F. Mikesell, *Foreign Investment in Petroleum and Mineral Industries* (Baltimore: Johns Hopkins University Press, 1971), pp. 435–36.

15. See the statements by Algeria, Iran, and Venezuela, *supra* n.1.

16. Ibid., also by the representative of Indonesia, U.N. Doc. A/PV.2214, pp. 49–50.

17. See the statement of J. Amuzegar of Iran, *supra* n.1 and the report of OECD's "Long-Term Energy Assessment" summarized in the *OECD Observer* no. 70 (June 1974): 7, 8. For a more detailed analysis of the effect of price rises and the "energy crisis" on future supplies, see Joseph Barnea, *The Energy Crisis and the Future* (New York: UNITAR Research Report No. 21, 1975).

18. UNCTAD Secretary-General, "The Impact of Recent and Prospective Price Changes on the Trade of Developing Countries," U.N. Doc. UNCTAD /OSG/52/Add.1, 4 Apr. 1974.

19. See statements by the representatives of New Zealand, U.N. Doc. A/PV.2211, p. 56, and Kenya, A/PV.2224, pp. 8–10.

20. See President Gerald Ford's address to the U.N. General Assembly, 18 Sept. 1974, U.N. Doc. A/PV.2234. See also statements at the U.N. General Assembly, 6th Special Session, by Secretary of State Kissinger, *supra.* n.2, representatives of Hungary, A/PV.2213, p. 27, Italy, A/PV.2218, and the United Kingdom, A/PV.2209, p. 117.

21. See the statement of J. Amuzegar of Iran, *supra* n.1. See also Walter J. Levy, "World Oil Cooperation or International Chaos," *Foreign Affairs* 52 (July 1974): 690–713; Hollis B. Chenery, "Restructuring the World Economy," *Foreign Affairs* 53 (January 1975): 242–63.

22. "Charter for an International Trade Organization," signed at Havana on 24 Mar. 1948: U.N. Conference on Trade and Employment, Final Act and Related Documents, E/Conf. 2/78, 1948.

23. UNCTAD Report of Experts, "Restrictive Business Practices in Relation to the Trade and Development of Developing Countries," U.N. Doc. TD/B/C.2/119, 26 Apr. 1973.

24. See R. N. Gardner, "The Hard Road to World Order," *Foreign Affairs* 52 (April 1974): 556. See also statements at the U.N. General Assembly, 6th Special Session, by the Philippines, U.N. Doc. A/PV.2221, p. 66 and by Italy, A/PV.2218, pp. 23–26. For a political analysis of producers' organizations and consumer groups, see Philip Connelly and Robert Perlman, *The Politics of Scarcity* (London: Oxford University Press, 1975), pp. 67–145.

25. See *Proceedings of United Nations Conference on Trade and Development (UNCTAD), 1973*, vol. 2, *The Development of International Commodity Policy*, U.N. Doc. TD/113, 3 Mar. 1972; Alton D. Law, *International Commodity Agreements* (Lexington, Mass.: D. C. Heath & Co., 1975).

26. An international group of experts in the United Nations concluded that "a price can be called 'fair', 'just', and 'equitable' as well as 'reasonable' as long as it does not perform extreme upward or downward gyrations which are caused by abnormal and transient conditions or serve no useful economic purpose." See UNCTAD "Study on Indexation," U.N. Doc. TD/B/503/Supp.1/Add.1, 5 July 1974, p. 4.

27. The United States position has become more favorable toward commodity price stabilization measures indicated by Secretary of State Kissinger in his major address to the Nairobi conference of UNCTAD on May 6, 1976. In particular, he approved buffer stocks for certain commodities exported by developing countries and suggested international financing for such stocks. He also advocated "producer-consumer forums" for "key developing-country commodity exports," New York *Times*, May 7, 1976, p. 12. See report of the prime minister of the United Kingdom to Parliament entitled "World Economic Interdependence and Trade in Commodities," May 1975, U.K. Cmnd. 6061 (H.M. Stationery Office), Part 3, paragraphs 6–8 and Annex 1.

28. UNCTAD Secretary-General, "An Integrated Program of Commodities," U.N. Doc. TD/B/C.1/166, 9 Dec. 1974 (and related supplements and annexes), "A Common Fund for the Financing of Commodity Stocks," U.N. Doc. TD/B/C.1/196, 6 Oct. 1975.

29. The problems of establishing and managing buffer stocks are summed up in the report of the prime minister of the United Kingdom, *supra* n.27, as follows:

11. However, the establishment and enlargement of buffer stocks is subject to at least four practical difficulties—

i. First there are the problems of controlling and managing buffer stocks. Some of these are technical difficulties. For instance it is far more difficult to manage a stock of a heterogeneous product such as tea than of, for instance, a metal; and some products such as coffee have proved more difficult than was expected to store in large quantities. In addition there are the inevitable problems of setting up and running an international organisation representing diverse interests.

ii. Secondly there is the difficulty of judging the requisite scale of the stocks. This involves taking a view of the degree of insurance that the members desire, and assessing the likely scale of world trade in the commodity and the size and frequency of fluctuations in supply and demand. These assessments may be difficult at a time when nobody can be certain whether the recent trend towards greater instability will continue.

iii. Thirdly there is the problem of finding the money. It has been calculated that for copper alone the value at present prices of a buffer stock representing 10 per cent of a year's output—a proportion which has proved inadequate for tin—could be £500 million. The financial problem would have to be tackled separately for each commodity. But if the policy worked well, the commodity would be sold when world prices had increased, so funds to build up buffer stocks could be regarded as finance for investment rather than for consumption.

iv. Finally, there is a problem of timing, since the stocks cannot be built up except when a surplus is available.

Nevertheless, in spite of the difficulties, there should be scope in many commodities for mutually beneficial cooperation between producing and consuming countries in buffer stock management. Indeed in many ways the provision of buffer stocks might be seen as one of the keys to smoothing the harmful fluctuations of supply, demand, and price that the world has been experiencing.

30. See UNCTAD studies on the indexation of prices in U.N. Doc. TD/B/503, 6 Aug. 1974; TD/B/503/Supp.1, 30 July 1974; TD/B/503/Supp.1/Add.1, 5 July 1974. The comments made in the text on indexation are based principally on these studies. See also M. Perez-Guerrero of Venezuela, *supra* n.1.

31. Prime Minister Harold Wilson, *supra* n.27, p. 4.

32. For a summary of the proposed schemes see n. B (pp. 23–27) and Annex 19, pp. 102–09 of United Kingdom report, *supra* n.27.

33. J. Amuzegar, "The North-South Dialogue: from Conflict to Compromise," *Foreign Affairs* 54 (1976): 562.

34. Article 13 of the "Charter of Economic Rights and Duties of States," U.N. General Assembly resolution 3281 (XXIX), 12 Dec. 1974; also published in *International Legal Materials* 14, no. 1 (January 1975): 251. U.N. General Assembly

resolution 3201 (S-VI), "Declaration on the Establishment of a New International Economic Order," 1 May 1974, paragraph 4.

35. Constantine Vaitsos, *Intercountry Income Distribution and Transnational Enterprises* (London: Oxford University Press, 1974). Walter A. Chudson, *The International Transfer of Commercial Technology to Developing Countries* (New York: UNITAR Research Report No. 13, 1971); Jack Baranson, *International Transfer of Automotive Technology to Developing Countries* (New York: UNITAR Research Report No. 8, 1971); R. H. Mason, *The Transfer of Technology and the Factor Proportions Problem* (New York: UNITAR Research Report No. 10, 1971).

36. Vaitsos, *supra* n.35, p. 139.

37. Walter A. Chudson and Louis T. Wells, "The Acquisition of Technology from Multinational Corporations by Developing Countries," U.N. Sales No. E.74.II.A.7, 1974, p. 48.

38. Covey Oliver, "The Andean Foreign Investment Code: A New Phase in the Quest for Normative Order as to Direct Foreign Investment," *Am. J. Int. Law* 66 (1972): 763, 780; Robert N. Seidel, *Toward an Andean Common Market for Science and Technology: Public Policy for Science, Technology and Industrialization in the Andean Group* (Ithaca, N.Y.: Cornell University, 1974).

39. U.N. General Assembly resolution 3202 (S-VI), "Programme of Action for a New International Economic Order," 1 May 1974, section 4; UNCTAD, "Preparation of a Draft Outline of an International Code of Conduct on Transfer of Technology," summary of replies from governments to the note verbale of the UNCTAD secretary-general of 20 Sept. 1974, U.N. Doc. TD/B/C.6/AC.1/3, 4 Apr. 1975.

40. A comprehensive account of the restrictive practices of concern to developing countries is contained in a report by the UNCTAD Secretariat, "An International Code of Conduct on Transfer of Technology," U.N. Doc. TD/B/C.6/AC.1 /2/Supp. 1, 25 Mar. 1975.

41. Ibid., p. 102.

42. UNCTAD, "Policies Relating to Technology of the Countries of the Andean Pact: Their Foundations: A Study by the Board of the Cartagena Agreement," U.N. Doc. TD/107, 29 Dec. 1971, in *Proceedings of UNCTAD Conference at its Third Session*, vol. 2, *Financing and Invisibles* (New York: United Nations), pp. 122–36. See also Oliver, *supra* n.38; Seidel, *supra* n.38.

43. See Chudson and Wells, *supra* n.37, p. 21.

44. Vaitsos, *supra* n.35, p. 136.

45. See UNCTAD report, *supra* n.40, pp. 85, 89. See also UNCTAD, "Restrictive Business Practices in Relation to the Trade and Development of Developing Countries: Report by the Ad Hoc Group of Experts of UNCTAD," U.N. Doc. TD/B/C.2/119, 26 Apr. 1973.

46. UNIDO, "Lima Declaration and Plan of Action on Industrial Development and Co-operation," U.N. Doc. ID/B/155/Add.1, 14 Apr. 1975.

47. UNIDO, "Long-range Strategy for UNIDO," U.N. Doc. ID/CONF.3/DEC.1, 10 Apr. 1975.

48. Netherlands Development Co-operation Information Service, *Internationale Samenwerking* 7, no. 10 (December 1974). The need for adjustment assistance in the United States is dealt with in Charles R. Frank, Jr., *Adjustment Assistance: American Jobs and Trade with the Developing Countries* (Washington: Overseas Development Council, 1973).

49. UNIDO, *supra* n.46.

50. "ACP-EEC Convention of Lomé, 28 February 1975," *International Legal Materials* 14, no. 3 (May 1975): 604.

51. Philippe de Seynes, "Address to the Symposium on International Needs and National Priorities," Stockholm, 8 Apr. 1975, UNITAR library, United Nations, N.Y.

52. U.N. General Assembly resolutions 1803 (XVII), 3016 (XXVII), 18 Dec. 1972, 2692 (XXV), 11 Dec. 1970, 3201 (S-VI), paragraph 4e, 1 May 1974, 3202 (S-VI), section 8, 1 May 1974.

53. In U.N. General Assembly resolution of May 1974, cited in n.1. The declaration refers to "the right of nationalization or transfer of ownership to its nationals, this right being an expression of the full permanent sovereignty of the State." It adds, "No State may be subjected to economic, political or any other type of coercion to prevent the free and full exercise of this inalienable right." Representatives of the market industrialized countries expressed their reservations to this clause, laying stress on the requirements of international law with respect to the grounds of nationalization and the obligation to pay compensation. For the legal implications, see Oscar Schachter, "The Evolving International Law of Development," *Colum. J. of Transnat'l. L.* 15 (1976): 1:16 and references n.54.

54. Summaries of national measures can be found in a series of reports by the secretary-general on Permanent Sovereignty over National Resources. See e.g. U.N. Docs. E/5425, 3 Oct. 1973; E/5170, 7 June 1972; and A/9716, 20 Sept. 1974. For problems of national control see Raymond Vernon, *Sovereignty at Bay* (New York: Basic Books, 1971); A. A. Fatouros, "The Computer and the Mud Hut," *Colum. J. of Transnat'l. L.* 10 (1971): 323–63; T. J. Farer, "Economic Development Agreements," ibid., pp. 200–41.

55. See article 2 of the "Charter of Economic Rights and Duties of States" adopted in U.N. General Assembly resolution 3281 (XXIX), 12 Dec. 1974. Six of the developed states, including the United States, expressly stated that they had reservations about this article, insofar as it might be construed to override international law, and could not therefore vote for the charter. Ten other states abstained. For an analysis of the present position in international law, see Burns Weston, "Inter-

national Law and the Deprivation of Foreign Wealth," in *The Future of the International Legal Order*, eds. C. E. Black and R. A. Falk, 5 vols. (Princeton: Princeton University Press, 1969-), 2: 36-182; Francisco Orrego Vicuna, "Some International Law Problems Posed by the Nationalization of the Copper Industry by Chile," *Am. J. Int. Law* 67 (1973): 711. See also Banco Nacional de Cuba v. Sabbatino, 376 U.S., pp. 398, 428-30, 1964.

56. See U.N. report, "The Impact of Multinational Corporations on the Development Process and on International Relations," prepared by a "Group of Eminent Persons" drawn from various parts of the world, U.N. Doc. E/5500/Add.1, 24 May 1974.

57. See, for example, Osvaldo Sunkel, "Big Business and Dependencia," *Foreign Affairs* 50 (April 1972): 517 ff.

58. See *Foreign Ownership and the Structure of Canadian Industry*, Report of a Task Force on The Structure of Canadian Industry (Ottawa: Privy Council Office, 1968); J. N. Behrman, *National Interests and Multinational Companies: Tensions among the North Atlantic Countries* (Englewood Cliffs, N.J.: Prentice-Hall, 1970).

59. Philippe de Seynes, United Nations under-secretary-general for economic and social affairs, "Address to the Southwestern Legal Foundation," Dallas, Texas, 13 June 1974, U.N. Doc. OPI/CESI Note/254, p. 3.

60. Ibid., p. 4.

61. For descriptions of this process, see T. H. Moran, "Politics of Economic Nationalism and the Evolution of Concession Agreements," *Proc. Am. Soc. Int. Law* (1972), p. 216; Moran, "Evolution of Concession Agreements in Underdeveloped Countries," *Vanderbilt J. Transnational Law* 7 (Spring 1974): 315. See also David N. Smith and Louis T. Wells, Jr., "Mineral Agreements in Developing Countries: Structures and Substance," *Am. J. Int. Law* 69 (1975): 560-90; Zuhayr Mikdashi, "National Resource Industries and the Multinational Firm" (New York University, Graduate School of Business Administration, Paper 75-04, January 1975).

62. See A. F. Lowenfeld, ed., *Expropriation in the Americas* (New York: Dunellen Publishing Co., 1971); Edith Penrose, *The Large International Firm in Developing Countries* (Cambridge, Mass.: M.I.T. Press, 1968); T. H. Moran, "The Politics of Oil, Coups and Costs," *Foreign Policy* 8 (1972): 129; Mira Wilkins, "The Oil Companies in Perspective," *Daedalus* 104 (Fall, 1975): 159-78; U.N. Secretary-General, "Report on Permanent Sovereignty over Natural Resources," U.N. Doc. A/9716, 20 Sept. 1974.

63. For a sweeping, muckraking account of the multinational corporation in developing countries, see Richard Barnet and Ronald Müller, *The Global Reach: The Power of the Multinational Corporations* (New York: Simon & Schuster, 1974). An interesting and more detailed study is Charles T. Goodsell, *American Corporations and Peruvian Politics* (Cambridge: Harvard University Press, 1974). See also U.S. Congress, Senate, Sub-committee on Multinational Corporations, I.T.T. and Chile: Hearing on, 83d Cong. 1st sess., 1973.

64. For example, the U.S. Negotiation Act of 1951, as amended.

65. Charles P. Kindelberger, *American Business Abroad* (New Haven: Yale University Press, 1969); Raymond Vernon, *Sovereignty at Bay* (New York: Basic Books, 1971).

66. See George Ball, ed., *Global Companies* (Englewood Cliffs, N.J.: Prentice-Hall Spectrum, 1975), pp. 65–66.

67. See U.N. report, *supra* n.56, Part 1, 1974, p. 22. See also Albert Hirschman, "How to Divest in Latin America," in *Princeton Essays in International Finance*, no. 76 (Princeton, N.J.: Princeton University, 1969).

68. J. K. Freeman, "Channelling Funds for Development," *Columbia J. of World Business* (Spring 1973): 66–71.

69. Gerald M. Meier, *Leading Issues in Economic Development: Studies in International Poverty*, 2nd ed. (New York: Oxford University Press, 1970), pp. 306–08.

70. U.N. report, *supra* n.56, pp. 36–38, 80–82.

71. See U.N. report, *supra* n.56, Part 2, comments by Senator J. K. Javits, pp. 91, 99 and by Irwin Miller, p. 115.

72. See Oscar Schachter, "Some Reflections on International Officialdom," in *International Organization: Law in Movement*, eds. J. E. S. Fawcett and Rosalyn Higgins (London: Oxford University Press, 1974), pp. 53–63.

73. See U.N. report, *supra* n.56, Part 3 on international machinery and action. In favor of an agreed code, see Eugene V. Rostow, "The Need for International Arrangements" in Ball, ed., *supra* n.66, pp. 156–58.

74. George W. Ball, "Proposal for an International Charter," in Ball, ed., *supra* n.66, pp. 170–71.

75. Ibid., p. 172.

76. See U.N. report, *supra* n.73.

77. See Joseph S. Nye, "The Longer Range Political Role of the Multinational Corporation" in Ball, ed., *supra* n.66, pp. 122, 141–42; Seymour J. Rubin, "The Multinational Enterprise at Bay," *Am. J. Int. Law* 68 (1974): 475, 487.

78. Henry Kissinger, *U.S. Dept. State Bull.* 71 (1974): 821, 829.

79. D. Gale Johnson, *World Agriculture in Disarray* (London: Macmillan, 1973), pp. 44–64. U.N. World Food Conference, "Assessment of the World Food Situation," U.N. Doc. E/CONF.65/3, section 2, 1974; Emma Rothschild, "Food Politics," *Foreign Affairs* 54 (1976): 285–307.

80. I. R. Manners, "The Environmental Impact of Modern Agricultural Technologies," *Ekistics* (Athens) 39, no. 230 (January 1975): 56–64.

81. Lester Brown and E. Eckholm, *By Bread Alone* (New York: Praeger-Overseas Development Council, 1974), pp. 146–72, 197–207.

82. T. T. Poleman, "World Food: A Perspective," *Science,* 9 May 1975, p. 515 says the most recent assessment of the world food situation prepared for the World Food Conference stated "what FAO's analysts have known all along—that those with money eat well wherever they may be, while the poor, be they in Bangladesh or Boston, suffer". See also A. Eide, "Planting Every Inch," *CERES* 8 (FAO publication), no. 1 (January–February 1975): 51–52.

83. World Food Conference report, "International Undertaking on World Food Security," U.N. Doc. E/CONF.65/20, resolution 17, pp. 14–15.

84. See Kissinger, *supra* n.78, p. 828.

85. Robert S. McNamara, "Let's Raise the Productivity of the Smallest Farms," World Food Resolution hearing before the Committee on Foreign Relations of the U.S. Senate (Washington, D.C.: Government Printing Office, 1974), p. 115.

86. Barbara Ward, "The Fat Years and the Lean," *The Economist,* London, 2 Nov. 1974, pp. 24–25.

87. World Food Conference report, *supra* n.83, resolution 2, "Priorities for Agricultural and Rural Development," 3d preambular paragraph recognizes "the vital importance . . . particularly of involving small farmers and landless labourers in the planning and operation of programmes aimed at improving their living standards and those of their families and at a more equitable distribution of income."

88. Brown and Eckholm, *supra* n.81, pp. 197–98.

89. Ibid., p. 199.

90. L. Brown and E. Eckholm, "Next Steps Toward Global Food Security," in *U.S. and World Development: Agenda for Action,* ed. J. W. Howe (New York: Praeger-Overseas Development Council, 1975).

91. Ward, *supra* n.86, p. 25.

92. "If men's inclination to self-interest makes their vigilance against one another necessary, their public sense of justice makes their secure association together possible," John Rawls, *A Theory of Justice* (Cambridge: Harvard University Press, 1971), p. 5. See also Aristotle *Nichomachean Ethics,* Book V, 6.

Name Index

Subject Index